ALIANZA ISLAMICA

Spanish Harlem's Islamic Odyssey

Rahim Ocasio

with

Juan Galvan

Cover design: Muhammad Yasir Bilal
Flag design: Shukrey (Fabel) Pabon

AlianzaIslamica.org

Published in the United States of America by Publishing Experts, LLC. Website: PublishingExperts.org.

.

ISBN 978-1-955021-00-5

... In some quarters, mouths still drop, and jaws become slack with amazement that a Latino could be a Muslim...

Rabim Ocasio, *Spring 1987*

Table of Contents

An Introduction

Juan Galvan

Thank you for purchasing this book and beginning your journey into the incredible story of Alianza Islamica! The origins and foundation of this now-influential Latino Muslim organization have long been overlooked and shrouded in shadows. Caught in the hearts and minds of its followers, no definitive and complete account has ever before been created. Now, you'll be taken on a profound and thought-provoking journey into the story of the Latino Muslim community – and how a few Latino teenagers in the middle of the civil rights movement gave rise to what would become, in a few short years, the most influential Latino Muslim organization in U.S history.

The relationship between Latinos and Islam has been a long, unique, and sometimes difficult one. From struggling with questions of identity and heritage to the wider feelings of the Muslim community, Latinos have faced an uphill battle in being accepted by other members of their faith and becoming a respected and valued part of the Muslim world. As much of an artful recounting of Alianza Islamica's origins, this book also seeks to shed light on the wider story of Latinos in Islam, reflecting on a rich and complex legacy which stretches back generations.

Alianza Islamica was more than just a building or a place to gather and worship. It continues to represent a movement, a push to spread the teachings of Allah to uplift and support those who need it most. In this sense, the backdrop of the civil rights movement could not be more fitting. When minority communities across the United States were calling for a voice and seeking freedom from discrimination and oppression, Alianza Islamica offered Latinos a real and tangible way to build their identities and draw strength in times of hardship. Their legacy continues to this day through the lives championed through their campaign to bring new communities into Islam both in Spanish Harlem and beyond.

Blending touching personal stories with real excerpts of writings and radio interviews with Alianza Islamica's founders, inside you'll witness an eye-opening look at the political, spiritual, and cultural landscape of the last half-century in the Latino Muslim community. You'll be taken on a tour of earlier organizations, including the Young Lords Party and the Nation of Islam. You'll explore the early divide between diverse cultures – as some Muslims believed that being a Latino follower of Islam was impossible. You'll face tough questions around heritage, racism, and what it means to embrace Islam. And you'll meet the incredible people who turned the dream of Alianza Islamica into a reality.

During a time when so many groups across the US were angered by the slow advancement of civil rights, along with more militant groups and solutions beginning to appear in minority communities, the rise of Islam in Spanish Harlem would soon send shockwaves throughout both the Puerto Rican community and wider Muslim world. Beginning with just a few teenagers who had a passion for Islam and the Word of Allah, nobody could have foreseen the heights which Alianza Islamica would rise within a few short years.

Many people may ask, why choose Islam as a Latino? How can converting to Islam enrich your life, give you purpose, and help you find direction? The impact this powerful and unifying faith has imparted is far-reaching. Islam offers its followers a keen sense of community and spiritual fulfilment. It paves the way for virtuous living with clear commandments to follow. While adopting Islam without abandoning or forgetting their Puerto Rican heritage may have been a challenge for some Latino Muslims, a unity between the Word of Allah and Latino culture has created a compelling and deeply satisfying foundation for a life of spiritual enlightenment and wellness under the guidance of our Creator.

Now, as Islam helped so many members of the civil rights movements all those decades ago by providing them with purpose and spiritual fulfilment, Alianza Islamica continues to empower and inspire disadvantaged people across the United States through their online presence, giving them hope through their struggles and helping them find their higher calling through Islam. During their early days, they even drew controversy for educating Muslims about HIV and AIDS, performing community outreach and counselling on a wide variety of topics including relationships and drug use. This comprehensive approach allowed them a unique way of practicing community outreach and helping those who might not have otherwise ever considered taking the path of Islam – or even stepping foot in a mosque.

Through Rahim Ocasio, one of the founding members and a first-hand witness to the earliest days of Islam in Spanish Harlem, you'll uncover an unparalleled account of the trials, struggles, and achievements of Latino Muslims in this turbulent time, preserving their legacy for generations to come. Carefully crafted to reflect the nuance and detail of Islam in Spanish Harlem, Rahim Ocasio draws on his firsthand experiences, memories, and decades of radio interviews and lectures to paint a truly engaging story.

The tale of Alianza Islamica has been a source of hope for many new Muslims like me. I met Yahya Figueroa, one of the founders, at an Islamic convention soon after embracing Islam in 2001, and I was immediately impressed by his stories of this small yet inspiring Latino Muslim organization from Spanish Harlem. He told me that he loves meeting Latino Muslims and that I needed to become a leader. I still reflect on that meeting often. I'm honored to be a part of this book that will educate Muslims from all walks of life about this important part of Latino Muslim history. The history of Latino Muslims in the United States did not begin post 9/11 – and most Latino Muslims have never even heard the beautiful history of the Bani Saqr from Newark, New Jersey in the 1970s.

In short, this book seeks to preserve the rich and vibrant story of Islam in the Latino community, committing to paper the events and stories which helped shape Spanish Harlem and the larger Latino Muslim community into what it is today. While countless lives come and go with no earthly record, *Alianza Islamica: Spanish Harlem's Islamic Odyssey* seeks to provide a thorough, detailed, and definitive look at the true story of this incredible movement, recounting the tales kept in the hearts and minds of its followers with a depth and clarity which will speak to your soul and show you what it was like to be a Latino Muslim 40 years ago.

A Brief History of Alianza Islamica: The Official Story

Rahim Ocasio

On Saturday, January 30th, Muslims and non-Muslims alike gathered in Houston, Texas, for the most highly anticipated event of the season: the grand opening of IslamInSpanish's *Centr Islamico,* the nation's new nexus for the propagation of Islam to Latinos.

Bright, sunny, nearly cloudless skies graced the sizable throng, most of them seated under a protective canopy while the rest stood bathed in the warmth of a Texas winter's sun.

While children frolicked in inflatable castles, the crowd was regaled with speech after speech, each discourse augmenting the event's auspiciousness, building up to the momentous climax when the blazing red ribbon at the center's entrance is severed, and curious eyes are finally sated.

It was a triumphal day, after all. Mujahid Fletcher, Abdullah Danny Hernandez, Isa Parada, Nahela Morales, Sandy Sakinah Gutierrez, and many others had concentrated their efforts to create, by the grace and mercy of Allah, something full of promise: a brand new center, physically stunning with mosaics, marble floors, decorative arches harkening to the grandeur of Cordoba, tastefully appointed masalah and lounge, and a high tech recording studio, all run by a cadre of Muslim workers of the highest caliber. There was much to celebrate.

I and my wife Faiza of 40 years, as well as Yahya Figueroa Abdul Latif, long-time director of Alianza Islamica, had made the trek and appeared to be the only New Yorkers.

Seating was at a premium, yet my wife had managed to find one in the back. I milled around a bit but eventually drifted back and found myself at her side. To my left, I saw Yahya, cutting a lonesome figure, sitting off to himself on the curb.

We three had unconsciously drifted toward the rear, observing, as it were, the proceedings from afar. We were a senior set, 60-somethings just now qualifying for discounts on movie tickets. Displayed before us was the riotous energy of youth, palpable in every part of the spectacle as a new generation dawned.

It was a study in contrasts. For decades ago, in the early 1990s, another Latino Muslim center opened in the heart of New York's Spanish Harlem, but to no fanfare, speeches, ceremonial ribbon cuttings, dignitaries, or honored guests. Neither newspapers nor television networks covered it, and news of its inauguration probably spread no further at the time than the curious glance of a passerby.

Over the next 12 years, Alianza Islamica became the largest and most influential Latino Muslim organization in U.S. history. Yet its story has lain buried for years in obscurity, hidden in the shadows of neglect and indifference.

It began with four teenage Puerto Ricans from the streets of Spanish Harlem.

Genesis

By the mid to late 60s, the Civil Rights movement's pacifism had given way to a restless and angry militancy that had grown impatient with the slow progress of social and economic reform for the nation's minority communities.

Seething inner-city neighborhoods erupted in an orgy of self-destruction. Riots broke out in major urban centers of the country like Watts in Los Angeles and Detroit, the latter being particularly devastating as entire blocks were obliterated and tanks were called in to restore order.

The foment gave birth to radically new types of organizations that adopted the socio-political narrative of liberation characteristic of the anti-colonial resistance raging throughout the world.

The Student Non-Violent Coordinating Committee (SNCC), the Black Panther Party, its Latin counterpart, The Young Lords Party, Movimiento Pro Independencia, El Comite, and the Puerto Rican Student Union were characteristic of this new type of organization which fostered an attitude and a rhetoric of resistance reinforced with images of armed revolutionaries prepared to defend their neighborhoods.

The Latinos of this era, especially those socially conscious and educated, were products of this new societal paradigm. More often than not, they were either sympathizers or active members of these new militant organizations.

In addition, Latinos of this ilk were generally distrustful and apprehensive toward government, aware of the oppressive and racist conditions endemic to American society, sympathetic to socialist solutions, and, if Puerto Rican, desirous of freedom and independence for the island of Puerto Rico.

Into this social milieu, four Puerto Rican teenagers from Spanish Harlem, *El Barrio*, the fabled iconic center of the Puerto Rican community in New York City, came of age.

They were Mark Ortiz, Freddie Gonzalez, John Figueroa, and this author, all living within five blocks of one another. Spanish Harlem at that time was a neighborhood in crisis, as were most in the country's inner cities, rotting from neglect and dissolution.

Enter The Young Lords Party

Founded in Chicago in 1968 by Cha Cha Jimenez as The Young Lords Organization, The Young Lords Party was an organization that focused on empowerment for Latino barrios with special emphasis on social and economic justice, health care, education, police injustice and abuse, tenants' rights, and Puerto Rican independence. They instituted free breakfast programs for needy school children long before the government caught on and presented themselves as a bulwark against the white-dominated establishment's oppressive policies. Their socio-political philosophy was socialistic based on Marxist-Leninist-Maoism.

The effect in *El Barrio* was electric and fired the imagination of restless youth. Mark was the first of us to join the movement, becoming a Young Lord at 14! By our late teens, we were all involved in some capacity. John and Freddie became involved with the Third World Students League, an ancillary arm of the Party dealing with organizing high schoolers. I became involved with two other subsidiaries of the Party, the CDC (Committee To Defend The Community), focusing on housing issues and PRSU, (Puerto Rican Students Union) aimed at college students.

These were the days of violent student protests and campus building takeovers and, on some nights, whether at the likes of the City College of New York or Columbia

University, the first early warning midnight watch was usually Freddie, John, and myself, a teen trio ranging from 15 to 18 years of age. And when we were not watching out for a police raid, we marched in street protests, demonstrating against colonialism, organizing high school students, and assisting tenants in organizing rent strikes.

In time, however, the movement began to lose its luster. It was not necessarily the revolution but the revolutionaries that were giving us pause. Internal conflicts and the spiritual vacuum created by drug use, drinking, promiscuity, and infidelity made us wonder what to expect of this brave new world re-made.

For a time, we were adrift, pursuing different paths, passing through different phases. It was a time of soul-searching and marching inexorably toward a destination we'd only know once we got there. In time, John and I were introduced to the Nation of Islam's teachings, a proto-Islamic movement popularized by Malcolm X.

The Nation of Islam countered the destructive effects of perceived Black racial inferiority with a narrative of Black racial supremacy. It embarked on a moral and economic upliftment program that transformed lives, turning degenerates, criminals, and disheveled ne'er-do-wells into disciplined, responsible, and dignified members of an active, vibrant organization.

The Nation of Islam members were a commanding presence in the neighborhood, while their modest, impeccably dressed women were equally as admired and highly respected. Another cause for this high level of respect was the knowledge that behind every man and woman of The Nation was a formidable security force: the FOI, the Fruit of Islam.

Trained by Master Moses Powell, the founder of the Sanuces Ryu Jujutsu system, the first martial artist to perform at the United Nations, and the first Blackamerican to train the DEA, the FBI, and the Secret Service in martial arts, the Fruit of Islam attained legendary status and was both respected and feared in the community.

It was an unquestioned ghetto maxim that Muslim women were always to be accorded the utmost respect and all carried an invisible yet clearly understood warning label; any breach was sure to bring heartache, headache, possible injury, or death.

However, as impressive as they were, John and I didn't join, settling instead to become members of The Five Percent Nation, an offshoot of The Nation of Islam, which shared much of the same teachings. Over time, its wild, heretical, and racist narrative of Black racial superiority and white demonization raised doubts and misgivings and was ultimately untenable in our multi-racial Latino culture. Our search continued.

One evening, while at an event celebrating the release of Puerto Rican political prisoner Carlos Feliciano on 116th St, we met one Abdullahi Rodriguez, one of the first Puerto Rican converts to Islam. With his counsel and guidance, our collective journey brought us eventually to Islam, all four of us becoming Muslims within two years of each other. John became Yahya, Freddie became Ibrahim, Mark became Abdus Salam, and Ray became Abdur Rahim. The Latino Muslim quartet was now complete.

First Steps in A New World

We were not the first Latinos to accept Islam in the city. Still, it was disconcerting to see that some of those who had preceded us — especially the ones closely associated with or members of predominantly African-American masjids — had become in effect, *crypto-Latinos*, totally subsumed into the African-American version of Islamic culture, refusing even to speak Spanish in the mosque. It was a jolting obliteration of identity; Willie Colon traded in for McCoy Tyner.

Many immigrant Muslims had trouble accepting Latinos as Muslims, some going as far as saying that the existence of a Latino Muslim was virtually impossible; no Latino could possibly be a Muslim. Also, due to Afro-Centric elements prevalent at the time, some of our African-American Muslim brothers handled Latinos' presence in the ummah awkwardly, especially when it came to dealing with the lighter-skinned and fair-haired.

To top it off, we had to deal with the perception in our Puerto Rican community that Islam was foreign to our culture, essentially *" a Black thing"* due to the notoriety of the Nation of Islam, and there were disturbing stories of stern Puerto Rican fathers ripping *khimars* (headscarves) off their daughters' heads.

For Latinos who had struggled to affirm their identity and preserve their dignity, these were clearly uncharted waters.

In 1974, we visited a Puerto Rican Muslim group in Newark, New Jersey, named Bani Sakr, an organization guided spiritually by Hajj Hisham Jaber, who led Malcolm X's funeral prayer. For the first time since we entered Islam, we were among other Muslims unashamedly Latino, proudly sporting names like Yusuf Padilla and Bilal Arce. A wedding there was a delight, feasting on sumptuous *arroz con pollo* to a soundtrack of percussive rhythms, *tumba y bongó,* an expression of ourselves that no longer looked foreign or alien, something our mothers could relate to. We now had a glimpse of what was possible and were determined to make it a reality.

The Islamic Party

In 1975, we joined the Washington, D.C-based Islamic Party of North America. The Islamic Party of North America was the first constitutionally based indigenous Islamic organization in the United States. IPNA's call was to establish Islam in all aspects of life: spiritual, economic, political, familial, and social. It also emphasized expressing Islam through civic engagement addressing problems of poverty and social and economic injustice. To that end, in addition to establishing a school and businesses, IPNA established an Oppressed People's Affairs Committee, programs for incarcerated Muslims and hunger (Feed the Hungry Month) and held symposiums on hunger and rape in the community.

It seemed to be the perfect melding of Islam with our pre-Islamic days of social activism, so we all enthusiastically became members. I went directly to Washington to work at its headquarters. Yahya, Abdus Salam, and Ibrahim remained in New York doing the Party's work of *dawah* (calling non-Muslims to Islam) and organizing.

By 1977, I was on the Guidance Council of the Party's Washington branch, but Yahya and the Party's New York contingent convinced me it was time to come home. We were reunited again in 1978. Unfortunately, not long after I rejoined the brothers, IPNA went into a period of turmoil and division that would eventually lead to a death spiral. We were left without a mooring. However, it was our first taste of a disciplined Islamic movement. The experience was to have a foundational influence.

The Spanish Mosque Debacle

In 1979, we became part of a pan-Latino group representing Muslims from Costa Rica, Puerto Rico, Panama, and Brazil. We held a series of meetings toward establishing the first Spanish-speaking masjid in New York City. In this setting, *khutbahs* (Friday sermons) and religious instruction would be given in our native tongue. Incidentally, it was here that we were introduced to a dynamic da'i (a caller to Islam) from Panama named Abdul Qadir, who was to become a life-long friend and unwavering supporter of the Latino *dawah* effort.

Unfortunately, Muslim leaders — immigrant and indigenous — viewed the project as divisive and damaging to the jamaat (the Muslim community). It met with considerable resistance and received no support from any established Muslim community. A sympathetic African-American Muslim brother allowed us to continue to meet at his apartment, but his local imam, on learning of this, ordered him to bar us from convening there. Shocked and disillusioned, the project lost momentum over time and was eventually abandoned.

Ibrahim Gonzalez Puts Latinos On The Map

After the Spanish Mosque debacle, Ibrahim Gonzalez left New York in the early eighties to take a job at ISNA (Islamic Society of North America) headquarters in Indiana. While there, he translated into Spanish a very popular dawah brochure of the time: *Islam at a Glance* or *Islam a un Vistazo*. As these were the days before desktop publishing, Ibrahim prepared the plates himself and readied them for publication. However, to his stunned disbelief, ISNA's leadership refused to print the brochure despite the virtual non-existence of any Spanish dawah materials at the time. His anger and frustration were evident in his frequent calls to me in New York.

Ibrahim returned to New York determined to change things around for Latinos and Latino Muslims and, in 1985, came up with a brilliant idea that was to change everything. He planned to stage an event highlighting Latin culture's Islamic legacy in a high-profile Fifth Avenue venue. Spanish Harlem's El Museo del Barrio, a museum dedicated to showcasing Latin culture, was the perfect choice. The theme was to be *Reclamando Nuestra Herencia Islamica* or Reclaiming Our Islamic Heritage.

Ibrahim, Yahya, and I put together the event, which featured the late T.B. Irving — a noted scholar, Quranic translator, and professor of Romance languages who passed away in 2002 — headlining a roster of speakers while our families chipped in to supply Latin cuisine. Ibrahim persuaded The Muslim World League to underwrite the event, and it was a huge success, drawing attendees from all over the country. Latino Muslims were finally emerging from the shadows.

However, an even bigger dividend was meeting two key men: Carl Askia El-Amin from the Bism Rabbik Foundation in Chicago and Daniel Ahmad Mena from Florida. They showed up with a duffel bag chock full of the first Spanish-language Islamic books we had ever seen.

After the event, a tri-city collaboration quickly developed, becoming the first iteration of Alianza Islamica. Its fruit was the first bilingual Islamic journal, also named *Alianza Islamica*, which the Bism Rabbik Foundation published quarterly, headed by Carl at the main office in Chicago. We chose this name to demonstrate solidarity, independence, and resistance to any attempts at co-opting. Ibrahim

Gonzalez and Daniel Ahmed Mena were associate editors, Maria Cartagena was the administrative assistant, Carl Askia El-Amin was the advertising and circulation manager, and Omar Abdur Rahim Ocasio was listed as its editor.

In the summer of 1986, Ibrahim Gonzalez was invited to Indianapolis to attend ISNA's annual convention, the same ISNA that had refused his constant requests some years earlier to print a simple Spanish dawah brochure. But now, representing Alianza Islamica, he addressed the seminar on Future Strategies for Dawah Work in North America along with a presentation of ISNA's Hispanic Dawah Program. By the grace and mercy of Allah, Ibrahim had managed to put Latino Muslims on the map. Latino Muslims were no longer an afterthought. The world had turned.

The tri-city collaboration lasted only about two years as technical, logistical, and financial obstacles eventually did in our essentially virtual organization.

Rebirth

One evening over thirty years ago, Yahya and I spoke of our dream of a dawah center in the heart of *El Barrio*, unassuming and unpretentious, an organic part of the neighborhood where anyone coming off the street would feel at home and comfortable while hearing the word of Allah. But by the early '90s, all we had to show for it were a string of starts and stops, booms and busts. But by the grace and mercy of Allah, the winds were about soon to change.

Yahya had long been interested in the field of drug intervention and, since the mid-1980s, had increasing contact with many Muslim converts in recovery. These

Muslims, in turn, referred others to Yahya. In time, a sizable group gathered around him. He began giving classes and lectures at his 12th Street duplex apartment, at a brother named Frenchie's apartment, and even on park benches. Spiritual retreats in the Poconos followed. The core of a nascent movement was emerging. All it needed was that final spark.

One day after Friday prayer in downtown Manhattan, I was approached by Yahya and his friend Khalil and asked if I would give them classes on *aqidah* (religious creed).

At first, it was just the two, then four, then six. More kept coming, brothers mostly and one sister, until they filled all the seats, then all available floor space. We then had to open another class on Sundays due to the increasing number of students. Something wholly unexpected was happening. These were the same newly minted Puerto Rican Muslims, straight out of rehab, that Yahya had been mentoring for some time. Now, with their lives turned around, they were hungering for more Islamic knowledge and appeared to be ready for more Islamic involvement.

In time, bonds of brotherhood developed, and Yahya and I agreed to seize the moment and formalize it by creating an organization. When the issue of a name came up, I suggested using the name mothballed and lying dormant since the mid-'80s (we were unaware at the time Carl was still publishing a journal under that name). All the pieces had come together. Alianza Islamica was re-born.

Getting To Work

By consensus, Yahya became the newly-resurrected Alianza's director and assumed the reins with an aggressive leadership style that quickly moved things along. Anxious to implement an Islamic-activist social agenda, he secured a storefront on 107th Street and Lexington Avenue, solidly in the neighborhood where we all grew up. All the early members and students from the aqidah classes were *Boricuas* from El Barrio. We had home-field advantage.

Yahya's priority was dawah, getting the message of Islam out to the people. Alianza's style was a hands-on, face-to-face street approach. He employed techniques to increase exposure and interest. To that end, there were periodic *caminatas*, where brothers and sisters, even whole families, would walk *en masse* down 3rd Avenue, Spanish Harlem's main street, to spark attention, curiosity, and, perhaps, some conversation. The storefront would periodically attract curious passersby who would come in and hear of Allah, The Most High's call to salvation in a calm, non-intimidating environment. Conversions grew at a steady pace, reaching nearly 100 families.

Alianza Islamica didn't confine itself to its immediate neighborhood in spreading its message. Alianza held events at Rutgers University, Cooper Union, Boricua College, and New York University (twice) and made radio program appearances. However, Alianza was distrustful of the mainstream media in general and kept it at a healthy distance.

Besides his innovative approach to dawah, Yahya pressed for programs that insured members and new Muslims' religious education. He enlisted scholars like the late Sharif Abdul Karim (may Allah have mercy on him), Ibrahim Abdul Aziz, and Ali Laraki. Realizing that many of the neighborhood's residents were disadvantaged, Alianza initiated GED, ESL, and employment programs to improve their social and economic situations. The educational programs were quite successful, with some going on to get Masters and Doctorate degrees.

The most successful employment program created was Alianza Islamica's branch of New York City's Muslim Security Force, which originated in Masjid At-Taqwa in Brooklyn and was led by Ali Abdul Kareem. During his visit to Manhattan's famous Upper West Riverside Church, Alianza Islamica provided security for multiple clients, most notably for Fidel Castro in September 2000. Health, nutrition, and even martial arts workshops rounded out a holistic approach to community development.

The object was to make a Latino Muslim part and parcel of the community, remove the stigma of the alien, and break down the barriers to the reception of Islam's message. Alianza Islamica made a concerted effort to Islamize our cultural elements to give our people familiar reference points.

An example was our Eid celebrations, held at times at community centers. Instead of the usual Middle Eastern or South Asian fare we were accustomed to eating at Muslim events, we went out of our way to showcase our cuisine. The sisters of Alianza, many of whom worked as hard or harder than any of the men, would spring to action with signature entrees like *arroz con gandules* and *pasteles*, and desserts like *flan* and *arroz con dulce*. My mother replaced the traditional *pernil* pork roast with a leg of lamb prepared and seasoned in the traditional way, effectively Islamizing our holiday dishes for all to see.

Music is a big part of Latino culture, especially of a tropical one like the Puerto Rican culture. Years ago, it was not an uncommon summer sight at a playground in *El Barrio* to see crowds gathered around 4 to 5 *congueros* beating Afro-

Boricua and Afro-Cuban conga rhythms into the night. Alianza decided that this part of our culture needed an Islamic expression as well. So, at Eids, skilled *congueros* Ibrahim, Yahya, and Muhammad Mendez entertained the crowds, the sounds of their *tumbaos, bombas, and guaguancos* emanating from the community center in an open invitation to all within earshot to a new Latin expression.

Drug And Prison Wars

In the early 1990s, the AIDS epidemic was growing rapidly, and American Muslim leaders were forced to confront drugs and HIV infection in their communities. But early reactions to this problem were positively medieval; Muslim deaths by AIDS were often deemed to be the wrath of Allah, and community members typically refused ritual washings of bodies in preparation for burial.

Yahya attended the Second International Aids Conference in Paris in 1986 and has always remained well informed about AIDS/HIV. On his initiative, Alianza Islamica became the first Islamic organization to ritually wash the bodies of Muslims who had died of AIDS. It also conducted outreach programs to educate Muslims and non-Muslims alike on AIDS and HIV.

Yahya recognized that if we were going to draw Muslims from our inner-city neighborhood, many would come broken and damaged by drugs and psychological and social ills. To address this, Alianza was instrumental in creating *Brothers in Recovery*, the first Islamic recovery group which is now well into its third decade.

Alianza Islamica also had to combat the problem of local drug dealers. Our next-door neighbors were drug dealers who were in turn protected by crooked cops.

Confrontation with these drug peddlers would, on occasion, get physical, and the threat of retaliatory violence was all too real. Yahya told me of a time he was armed, walking steadily toward a confrontation with drug pushers, struggling to maintain a brave face while his hands were shaking from fear.

Yahya insisted that Alianza Islamica have good, cooperative relations with law enforcement. This proved very advantageous; with persistence and a big helping hand from Captain Robert Curley and the officers of the 23rd Precinct, Alianza successfully cleared the block of drug dealers.

Yahya always maintained that Alianza Islamica should take a proactive approach in dealing with incarcerated Muslims' problems. In the 1990s, during Mayor Rudy Giuliani's administration, an inmate blood feud erupted in the correctional facility on Rikers Island between the Latin Kings, the Bloods, and incarcerated Muslims. An epidemic of slashings had gotten out of hand. Yahya had connections with the leadership of the Latin Kings and, on behalf of Alianza Islamica, was able to broker a truce. Mayor Giuliani was so impressed that he offered Yahya the chaplaincy but could not provide him with flexible hours. Nevertheless, the incident established Yahya and Alianza Islamica's credibility as a major player in future prison negotiations and disputes.

Latinas in Crisis

One of Alianza's most distressing problems was the inordinately large cases of spousal abuse, overwhelmingly in marriages of Latinas to Arab husbands. The evident predilection for Latinas among immigrant Arabs, especially for those with American citizenship like Puerto Ricans, and the disturbing incidents of verbal and physical abuse forced Alianza to be a haven offering assistance and badly needed counseling services.

Unfortunately, in recent meetings with Latino Muslim leaders, it has become evident that this problem persists unabated and remains a significant issue in the Latino Muslim community.

Unsung Heroes

Alianza was blessed with a cadre of dedicated members who bought totally into the dream of making a Latin expression of Islam a reality and seeing it spread among our people. Shukrey (Fabel) Pabon, Mustafa Rivera, Peter Robasa, Sa'id Concepcion, Maryam Roman, Safia Figueroa, Mikail (Miguel) Marrero, and Abdullahi Rodriguez, among others, were the indispensable cogs that kept Alianza's engine running.

There is one, though, that deserves special mention: Amin (Frenchie) Madera. Though terminally ill with AIDS, he was our gatekeeper, the one you could always rely on to open Alianza's doors in the morning and to close them at night. He was available for all asked of him, was never cross, always even-tempered, and would always greet you with a smile. Humble, unpretentious, and a devoted servant of Allah, he was the best of us and represented the best of Alianza Islamica.

Pluralism In Practice

Though the vast majority of Alianza's members were Puerto Rican, the organization could count on several non-Latinos whose contributions were invaluable. Chief among them was Shaikh Shair Abdul Mani, a brilliant Afro-American polymath who grew up in Spanish Harlem, was fluent in Spanish, and was the organization's public relations officer. He brought an urbane sophistication, professionalism, and polish to a somewhat gritty organization. Muhammad Omerjee was a Burmese gentleman of Gujurati descent who always sought ways to work more efficiently. And Christie Aziza Zimmerman, a German-American firebrand with an indomitable spirit who, along with her husband Shukrey, were pillars of unflinching support.

Finally, of all the imams in the city, no one has been more staunch in his support than Imam Talib of the Muslim Brotherhood Mosque. He has been there for us in life and death, being the first to offer his services in caring for our dead. May Allah reward him for being a friend to the oftentimes friendless.

La Mezquita Del Barrio

In the mid-90s, Alianza accepted an invitation by a prominent Indian Muslim to move to a building nearby. He, too, had a problem with drug dealing tenants from the notorious Jamaican Posse and was hoping to get some assistance in getting rid of them. There Alianza established *La Mezquita del Barrio*, the first Latino community-based masjid on the East Coast, perhaps the country, that we were aware of. Finally, there was now a place where Latino-Muslims could hear khutbahs that spoke to their reality, ending years of feeling left out and marginalized.

The *Mezquita's* establishment was a milestone for us as it had taken the storefront center concept to its logical conclusion. We could now serve Latinos and Latino Muslims in a way the Islamic Cultural Center just ten blocks could never hope to. Ibrahim Abdul Aziz became the titular imam of the masjid, responsible for Friday lectures and spiritual guidance.

Alianza had made at its outset the conscious decision not to mimic the traditional masjid model prevalent in the city at the time. That is why the founders established a dawah center with a director at its head rather than a masjid. Alianza's success, however, made the establishment of a masjid inevitable.

Unfortunately, relations between Alianza and the building owner deteriorated, and though Alianza effectively expelled the drug peddlers from his building, the owner-initiated eviction proceedings. In 2000, Alianza moved to Alexander Avenue in The Bronx but torn from its roots, it was never the same. A slow, inexorable decline ended in 2005 with flames reducing to ashes its final resting place.

A New Era, A New Dawn

Back in Texas, the ribbon was finally cut, and visitors were now pouring into the new center. The new day had arrived. Yet for we who were approaching the twilight of life, it was a time to reflect. A journey that began with four *Boricua* teenagers 47 years ago had brought us to this day. But we were no longer a quartet. Abdus Salam left for Riyadh at the end of the first Gulf war. As the self-titled *Latin from Manhattan*, he is reported to have brought a great number of GIs to Islam, and Ibrahim Gonzalez, the youngest of us and an innovative, determined pioneer, died suddenly in his sleep a couple of years ago, may Allah envelop him in forgiveness and mercy.

But there is much reason for hope, for we see in the leaders of IslamInSpanish and the leaders of Latino movements who converged there for the event the steely fiber necessary to take this effort to the next evolutionary level.

Each of the tribes and nations Allah has created represents bricks in the wall of humanity. Latino Muslims form bricks in the wall of the ummah. If our people are subservient and lack confidence, dignity, or self-esteem, we are no better than bricks made of substandard materials. And if we do nothing to correct this condition, then we are no better than crooked, unscrupulous contractors placing in the edifice of the ummah bricks that will not support the weight and jeopardize the integrity of the entire structure.

But if we are confident and believe in Allah and His Messenger (peace and blessings be upon him), we should realize that Allah has not only honored us by bringing us to Islam, but that we are also the spiritual and cultural heirs to the best of Andalusian civilization. We would respect and demand respect and let nothing or no one impugn our dignity. If needing to accept any assistance, we would do so only on our terms and not based on what looks good in someone else's annual report. These indeed would be bricks of the highest quality, purity, and strength.

I wish to end with an excerpt from an editorial I wrote for the premier issue of our journal *Alianza Islamica*, Spring 1987:

" We are not merely interested in starting a new cultural phenomenon of halal tacos and Islamized aguinaldos. Nor are we interested in the parochial, chauvinistic rise of a subject people to dominance and superiority at the expense of others. On the contrary, we, inshallah, will dedicate ourselves to making Latinos aware of their birthright as vicegerents of the Lord of the Universe, what that position entails, and how the proper execution of their responsibilities can lead to true happiness in this life and in the hereafter...

...In this country, Latino Muslims are still few in numbers, but they are raising a considerable share of eyebrows when spotted on subways, at department stores, or while strolling through the park with their families. In some quarters, mouths still drop, and jaws become slack with amazement that a Latino could be a Muslim...

"...When non-Muslims, curiosity aroused, ask us about our religion, oftentimes there is a titillating streak of excitement in the air. The lure of the daring, the bold, the new is there to awaken a whole new generation to their lost heritage. We, therefore, urge our readers to...plunge headlong into the real-life human drama where the souls of men are at stake; we urge you to spread this message by word, deed, and example. And, finally, we urge all to band together to recreate that beautiful sense of pop-eyed wonder as a people, heretofore despised and rejected, assume their rightful place in the family of man as vicegerents of the Lord and Master of all the worlds."

Note:

The version you just read is the enhanced version from my blog, which includes additional content not included in the Islamic Monthly article of March 16, 2016 due to their 4,000-word limit. It is the most comprehensive account of the evolution and history of Alianza Islamica.

A Lifetime Of Reclaiming Our Islamic Heritage

February 17, 2017, Alianza Islamica

By Yahya Abdul Latif Figueroa

Director, Alianza Islamica

Part 1 of 3

Beginnings and starting points are always difficult to determine and become obscured in the pages of bygone days. How and when movements and ideas bloom is never easy to pinpoint. Historical studies of the same period rarely agree on critical issues. Nonetheless, the following lines hope to set the record straight on an urgent matter and provide an accurate picture regarding the spread of Islam among Latinos and the birth of the first circle that exclusively worked among Spanish speakers in the US.

The 1960s and 70s were decades of momentous turmoil and upheaval among minority communities in the US. It was the age of reclaiming lost identities, the assertion of ethnic pride, and the rediscovery of cultural roots. It was also a time of soul-searching and the discovery of new spiritual paths and religions. Small groups of minority American Blacks and Latinos turned to Islam. These were the days of the Nation of Islam, and movements such as the Moorish Science Temple, the Ahmadiyya, and the Ansarullah community. Also, legions of American Muslims embraced authentic Sunni Islam due to the influence of the late Malcolm X, rejecting Elijah Muhammad's heretical claim to prophethood and asserting the belief in Muhammad (PBUH) as the seal of the Prophets. Uniquely Sunni groups arose against this background giving rise to small independent communities working within their inner-city neighborhoods. The most well-known was the Dar-ul-Islam Movement at Herkimer Place in Brooklyn and the Mosque of the Islamic Brotherhood (MIB) in Harlem.

In 1987, a small Latino group of Muslims formed Alianza Islamica, and its nucleus of members gathered and set forth a plan to incorporate and open a mosque/cultural/dawah center. During the decade of the nineties, its heyday, it had become a well-oiled machine, eventually establishing La Mezquita del Barrio, the first one of its kind we were aware of.

Alianza was born in Spanish Harlem, the very heart of the Latino community in New York City. It was no coincidence that Alianza took root in the very center of one of the oldest and most iconic Latino communities in the US. From the very start, Alianza sought to combat the social conditions faced by our people with the dynamic spiritual teachings of Islam. Based in the center of Hispanic intellectual and cultural life, Alianza participated in a bold and fresh manner. Not only did we dialogue with other faiths, but we challenged the various ideologies and social movements of the time presenting an Islamic alternative.

It was a spiritual-cultural center aiming to revive and rediscover the soulful treasures of Al Andalus. In its most successful period, we served approximately 100 families, many of them single disenfranchised young people. Hundreds of other transients were touched profoundly as well. We believed that we had a unique approach to Islam and that the cultural glory of Andalusia was extremely relevant to our people's needs. Many of our most supportive participants were non-Latinos, as our center provided refuge for all seeking help. Our neighborhoods suffered from much of the dysfunction of urban life, discrimination, and lack of opportunity, most often the product of discriminatory policies. Thus, Alianza had a singular mission to present Islamic teachings against this very troubled background.

We sought to bring a down-to-earth vision of Islam, confident that this message could alleviate the problems we faced. We offered family counseling and community support. Different courses presented the basic Islamic sciences, Fiqh, Quran, Hadith, and classics of spirituality, especially those of Al Andalus. Due to the community, we served, many came with troubled pasts. Alianza sought to help this population and aid in the recovery of broken souls and families. Wholesome companionship, brother and sisterhood distinguished our efforts. For many, conversion to Islam had brought trauma to their families, and we sought to fill that gap. We celebrated the Islamic holidays offering communal meals and joyous occasions for those with no extended families. Conversions to Islam occurred regularly, and community life pulsed with all its customary trappings: communal prayer, weddings, celebrations of birth, and death's solemnity. In addition, Alianza reached out to the Harlem community and participated in community affairs with their non-Muslim neighbors.

Alianza Islamica continued to function until 2005, long after 9/11, and for various reasons, the center came to a halt. Many of the members recall fondly those "golden days" of our activities and long to become active once again, seeking a fresh start.

Nonetheless, Alianza is delighted by IslaminSpanish's Centro Islamico and embraces it as an extension of our humble beginning. We hope it enhances the basic message of Alianza and becomes a force for the unique spiritual culture of historical Andalus, while skillfully avoiding the excesses and failures of many contemporary Islamic movements. We also hope that it forges a genuinely unique movement to transmit the timeless guidance of Allah, the Most High, as embodied in the paragon of books, al Qur'an, and the Sunnah of His Prophet (PBUH) among Latinos. Let us boldly proclaim our timely vision based upon our glorious past and new opportunities that are ours here in the US.

Finally, Alianza would like to acknowledge the inspirational debt owed to the early American Sunni, primarily African-American communities of New York; the Dar ul Islam Movement and the Mosque of Islamic Brotherhood, as well as the foundational influence of the DC-based Islamic Party of North America in our special mission to the Hispanic community.

A Seminary Student Interviews Rahim Ocasio

Bilal Acevedo is the grandson of Rahim Ocasio. This interview occurred in 2018.

Bilal Acevedo:

You mentioned the Islamic Party as being the first formal Islamic movement-oriented organization you all were apart of. So how did Islamic Party affect you all in terms of the programs, the methodology, or the form in which you may have done your Dawah?

Rahim Ocasio:

Okay. Very important to understand that Alianza Islamica in its bylaws and its approach owes a lot to the Islamic Party of North America. You can't discuss that unless you address that. I mean, ideologically speaking.

Bilal Acevedo:

Do you say Alianza owes?

Rahim Ocasio:

Oh yes, absolutely. If you looked at the bylaws of Alianza Islamica for their 501c3 organization, they are taken right out of the Islamic Party's constitution in North America. You have to understand that both me and Yahya were part of the Islamic Party of North America before Alianza Islamica was established. So, the Islamic Party of North America, again, as I said before, was an extension of that movement mentality, an outgrowth of the movement mentality that existed among the early Muslim converts in the '60s and '70s.

Remember that many of the people who became Muslims, and I am talking about not specifically the Afro-Americans, became Muslims because of Malcolm. And Malcolm was definitely a radical and an activist. He was considered revolutionary and influenced many. No question.

The Islamic Party itself was kind of an amalgam, at least the constitution. Ideologically, the constitution is an amalgam of the Jamaati Islami and the Ikhwan. The brothers got together and started looking at both constitutions to see how they can adapt it to create a national organization. It is an astonishing document.

It was the basis for the Islamic Party and made it the first constitutionally based indigenous Muslim organization that had a nationwide organizational plan. It's an astounding document, which I think they've uploaded to the site now. I asked Juan to upload it to the site because it is significant when speaking about Alianza Islamica. I was the only one of the Latino brothers who went to the Islamic Party headquarters in Washington. Yahya continued the work up here, but he never went down other than to visit. He didn't spend time with the brothers down there nor participated firsthand in the program and the work. It was your grandmother and I who did that.

As Islamic movements at that time, the Jamaati Islami, the Ikhwan Islamic specifically, were community service-based, it was a logical that the Islamic Party and eventually Alianza Islamica would be that way. That was not exclusive to Islamic organizations because the Young Lords Party and the Black Panther Party were also like that. The difference was that now it was an Islamic organization doing it.

Bilal Acevedo:

Okay. So, you mentioned that you all had issues with ISNA. It was ISNA that you all had issues with, right?

Rahim Ocasio:

It was ISNA. The issue we had with ISNA, which led to Alianza Islamica being created, is talking about a different time. We are talking about circa 1985. In 1985, Ibrahim came up with the idea of having an event at Museo del Barrio which you read about in the article, and after that the word got around. All of a sudden, we were on the map. I mean, before that, Latinos were ignored. Now, all of a sudden, we could be useful. So, we got a request which was kind of an insult. They wanted us, me, Ibrahim, and Yahya, to come to an ISNA conference and to give a talk on Latino dawah, but they wanted all of us to submit our speeches in writing, which they were going to collate and make into a dawah handbook to be published under their auspices.

Now the reason that's an insult was that we were quite aware that Ibrahim had been working at ISNA for the last few years before returning to New York and that they were having funding troubles. Organizations that were regularly funding them, overseas organizations, and institutions, felt that they were wasting their money, and they were not doing what they were supposed to. We believed that the attempt to have it published under their auspices was just a funding scheme because they would publish it and give us no credit whatsoever. They would then turn around and use that to get more funding, which would probably go nowhere. In other words, they were trying to use us.

They kept calling me, then calling individuals who were participating in this effort. We realized that we had to present a unified face. I suggested the word Alianza

Islamica. Sometimes that is debated because I've heard somebody say that Ibrahim did. Still, I recalled being the one who said we should call ourselves Alianza Islamica to provide a unified front Now, when they contacted us, we would speak as one voice and couldn't pick us apart. That is how that came about.

The issue of co-opting for us was a big deal. We did not want to be co-opted by any major organization at that time, especially one like ISNA. They had repeatedly ignored Ibrahim while he was working there, when he tried his darnedest to get a Spanish leaflet printed up for dawah at a time when there was not a single sheet of paper in Spanish dedicated to Latino dawah, absolutely none. Yet he was repeatedly ignored. So, we were not going to give them any satisfaction at all. We were going to continue doing our work and let them do whatever they wanted to do.

Bilal Acevedo:

Okey-doke. So, you've mentioned in the article, that there was a journalist you jointly worked with on the journal called Alianza Islamica, that was published by the Bism Rabbik Foundation. What kind of content did that contain?

Rahim Ocasio:

The site should have a copy of it. It was written in a paper format, and it was not like a magazine. That was very popular. Like The Nation, which had Muhammad Speaks, a newspaper, and the Islamic Party which had The Al-Islam Journal, and we had Alianza Islamica. It was written in a journal format and was bilingual. You could turn it around for Spanish. I only have one. I think we had two or three copies of it published before we stopped. I have scanned it and made it into a PDF. On the article, on my blog, you have a picture of it, at least its front cover.

It dealt with Islamic dawah, the history of Spain, and other subjects. It was relevant to the target audience that we wanted to reach, encouraging, and making people aware of Latino Muslims and their history, et cetera.

We published maybe two issues. It was called Alianza Islamica. If you had an organization in those days, you were supposed to have a journal. That was the thought at the time. When we established Alianza Islamica, it was called Somos. It was not as elaborate as Alianza Islamica or the Al Islam Journal. It was four pages at the most, more like a newsletter. The others were journals.

We had no expertise at all in layout and publishing. That was all done in Chicago by Carl Askia Al Amin and his wife in the Bism Rabbik Foundation, who published it in Chicago, but we submitted the edited articles. Once submitted, it was put together in Chicago by the Bism Rabbik foundation.

Bilal Acevedo:

Okay. So, the next thing was, did you all have any other classes before the pivotal class that you mentioned?

Rahim Ocasio:

Yeah, but I was not a part of those. That is where Yahya comes in because those brothers that Yahya was bringing me… Remember there's no Alianza Islamica yet, and I thought nothing was going on.

But there really was something going on, but I was not aware of it. Yahya had already been having classes gathering people around him, unbeknownst to me. They would meet at his apartment downtown or have retreats in the Poconos. They would meet anywhere, even on park benches.

All this was going on, and I was unaware. Then he came to me saying that he wanted to have aqidah classes with him and a brother named Khalil. I started giving those classes, and he started to bring people one by one, two by two, and then all of a sudden, it became a tsunami.

Bilal Acevedo:

Okay. Did you feel Alianza's focus was more on establishing a Latino Muslim identity, or did you feel it was more on this communal development? Or did you feel like there was not necessarily a distinction, your thinking was that they go hand-in-hand?

Rahim Ocasio:

Yes. It was hand-in-hand. The point is, is that we wanted to bring the word of Allah to the people, to our people, who were underserved. It is clear that at that time, Latinos were forgotten. Even the dialogue about race was centered more on the African-Americans, not so much on Latinos. So much so that it was like pulling teeth to get these major organizations even to notice we were there. So, the whole idea of trying to make up for the fact that we were an underserved community had a lot to do with that.

Bilal Acevedo:

Okay. What did you think was unique about Alianza in terms of the dawah approach?

Rahim Ocasio:

Well, just the fact that it existed was unique. There was nothing like it. I mean, absolutely nothing. Here's an organization that wants to bring Islam to an underserved, predominantly Latino community, very poor, and not only bring them Islam but also to bring them services, the things that would enrich and enhance the people: GED classes, English as a Second Language, health, job training, All to give to the community, attempting to show that Islam is a religion of service, not just take, take, take, but give, give, give, as well. There was nothing like it. Not even close.

We were doing things the Afro-Americans were not doing, not at that level. So yes, it was very unique. There is nobody doing it now. There is someone attempting to do it, for example, Esperanza, in Passaic. And even then, he says that he's doing it because he was inspired by the example of Alianza Islamica. So, there's nothing like that now.

I mean, you have a specialized project like Embrace which is trying to help converts, follow up, and keep them in Islam. But they are individual programs. You have IslamInSpanish which gives dawah and publishes literature, et cetera. But the actual caliber of service that we are talking about here hadn't been done before, not with Latinos, not on that level and not since. So, it's quite unique.

Bilal Acevedo:

Every organization has their pillar thing that really made it what it is. What do you think were those pillars that made Alianza what it was… like the biggest and best programs that they offered?

Rahim Ocasio:

One of the biggest things was the leadership of Yahya Figueroa. A large amount of the success of Alianza Islamica, what made Alianza Islamica the way it is, is Yahya Figueroa. I mean, not only him; you also had some really, good, dedicated workers. I mean, exceptional people. Just like those guys that I mentioned in the article that I cited, every one of those people was top notch. I singled out one because that guy was outstanding. Amin Madera. There was nobody like him. I mean, he was like the person you could always rely on. He would be there to open the doors and close up, and, for anything you wanted, he was always there. There was nobody like him.

When you have a good program and set your standards high, you attract certain people. And people are what made Alianza Islamica. And not only the guys, but it was also the women. So, it's the personnel. And then you must look at the top, too. A person who was an astounding leader, a person who got things done, Yahya was like that. When you look at these kinds of things, look for the people and look at the leadership. And with leadership, you must single out one in particular, and that's Yahya.

Bilal Acevedo:

Okay. Did Alianza have an emphasis like The Nation on buying local and keeping things in the community? Did Alianza have the same emphasis?

Rahim Ocasio:

Well, we did try to start businesses. The issue of dealing with people's real problems is what you are talking about. People need jobs, people need work, people need economic stability. If they do not have that, everything else is really shaky. There was a strong emphasis on getting people to work. Alianza itself developed a security agency. Many of the brothers were part of it. They also tried to start other ventures. It is the old mantra of The Nation, "Do for self." You must have some kind of economic engine going to get some self-sufficiency. It's not easy to do, but you must try. They tried to take it to another level by recognizing that economic stability is an issue and trying to address it.

Bilal Acevedo:

Okay. Alianza established, a dawah center first, and then a masjid was started, right? So, when did Alianza relocate that mosque? I was not quite sure about that.

Rahim Ocasio:

It was just across the street. Alianza Islamic had cleared out the drug dealers from 107th Street. Then a Muslim doctor who had a building across the street invited us to come over. They had space there that was big enough to establish a masjid. We did not have a masjid. People could pray there, but it was basically a dawah center, not a masjid. Across the street, we could have a masjid if we cleared out the drug dealers. He wanted our services to rid him of the drug dealers in exchange for a space big enough to establish a masjid. And that is how we got La Mesquita del Barrio, the first masjid in a Latino neighborhood.

Bilal Acevedo:

Okay. What happened between you all and that landlord?

Rahim Ocasio:

The landlord was a slumlord. After Alianza was successful in clearing out the drug dealers from his building, he did not repair anything. He was letting it go to pot. There were disputes and complaints, possibly some withholding of rent, because he was not fulfilling his end of the bargain. He made the place unfit to live, unfit to be inhabited. He forced Alianza out after he got what he wanted. He didn't take care of the building as he was supposed to. Eventually, the decision was made that it was an untenable situation, and Alianza was forced to leave. Then he parades down Madison as Grand Marshall of the Muslim Day Parade.

Bilal Acevedo:

Okay. So, what were the difficulties when you all went to the Bronx? Because once you guys went to the Bronx, you mentioned that things started to die slowly?

Rahim Ocasio:

When we were in del Barrio, we were on home turf. People lived nearby. It was a community. When we moved to the Bronx, it was no longer a community. Our connections were severed. We were cut off from our base, and it started to make a difference when people had to commute. It was no longer a neighborhood operation.

That is why I wrote the words "torn from your roots." All those connections, everything that we had was based in Spanish Harlem. We went into a totally different place where there were no connections whatsoever. Nobody lived nearby. It was very different.

Bilal Acevedo:

You were literally a neighborhood organization outside of your neighborhood.

Rahim Ocasio:

Yes. Everything we did was based on our community, and now we were not there anymore. It was not the same. People could just walk in off the streets. Things started to change a lot. It was not automatic. It was slow, but inevitable.

Bilal Acevedo:

What was the biggest effect do you think Alianza had on the community?

Rahim Ocasio:

Well, people knew us. At that time, we did not have any issues with terrorism or anything like that. I mean, we did not have to justify ourselves in that kind of way. People got to know us as people who are part of the community. I mean, we were very Boricua. There was no doubt about that. You could see that in the way we celebrated our Eids. We wanted to make it clear that we were not really foreign.

That was a big issue for us. This whole idea, when we first became Muslim, of our own people thinking that we were alien, that we adopted some kind of alien ideology, or that we were following the Morenos (Blackamericans), which was a big problem with some of our parents. A lot of us were young. I was 19. There were not a whole lot of older people accepting Islam. Most of us were young people. So, we did this often while still living with our parents. We knew how it was and how they reacted to this, that we were not really Latinos. That we were following Morenos or Arabs, Turks, or whatever.

We wanted to portray to our people a Latin expression of Islam. And Alianza Islamica was that in many ways. There was a strong emphasis on making Islam Latino, making it our own just like every other nation has done. There was a big emphasis on that.

I think the most significant impact besides the services was the removal of cultural and psychological barriers to accepting Islam's message. At that time, those cultural barriers existed. They exist now but for different reasons, terrorism, all that other stuff. But at that time, it was a cultural thing. For example, Central Americans, Mexicans, are even more hard-nosed than Puerto Ricans, because Catholicism is more firmly entrenched there. They would not even speak to me. When I would give dawah on Columbia Road, in the Salvadorean neighborhoods in Washington DC, they did not even let me get a word out. They would just say, "Yo soy Catolico." and just keep on walking. You would not get that kind of reaction in a Puerto Rican neighborhood. There are barriers to even getting into a dialogue. These barriers exist, and it is essential to do things that will weaken that barrier or eliminate it so that a dialogue can exist.

Bilal Acevedo:

Yes. Okay. I am trying to think. There was a question I had in my mind, that, just let me for a second. Okay. Those are the questions that I had. So, this is more of a personal question just between you and me more than anything else. But when I talk to Yahya, what do you think are the most important things I should ask him about?

Rahim Ocasio:

What you asked me. I mean, basically.

Bilal Acevedo:

The same things?

Rahim Ocasio:

Yes. You will get his perspective. I mean, what you will be able to get more of what was actually happening with those brothers that he was talking to before they came to me. What got them? How he was able to get them? That would be an important question to ask him.

Bilal Acevedo:

Right.

Rahim Ocasio:

The engine of Alianza Islamica was Yahya's leadership and those brothers he brought in. So, you should ask more about those brothers, and ask what made Alianza move. People made Alianza move. So that is an important question to ask him.

Bilal Acevedo:

How do you think Hanuti influenced you when you were in DC?

Rahim Ocasio:

When I was in DC? If Hanut influenced me? I was influenced in New York.

Bilal Acevedo:

Oh sorry.

Rahim Ocasio:

I went to classes in Brooklyn to see him. He had a huge influence on me. When we sat down at Hanuti's classes, he made me feel like I never knew Islam. And by the time I was going to classes with him, I had been a Muslim for almost 14 years, yet I felt like I had never known the din, like I had to take shahadah all over again. It was just a completely refreshing approach to Islam. The way he viewed things. The fact that he has gone hurts because there's so much, I would like to ask him. But yes, his approach was so refreshing. What would I call it? Minority fiqh? I mean it. It has had a huge influence on me to this day.

Bilal Acevedo:

I mean, this is just what I think from talking to you just personally, I do not think you would be right now all into this maqasid stuff and Maliki fiqh if you hadn't met Hanuti.

Rahim Ocasio:

I don't know if that's true or not, but his classes were almost one eye-opener after another. Like "What? What? Really, what?" You wind up saying that over and over again. He was a great debunker. He'd make you look in different directions and make you think. He would make statements and then present the evidence to back it up, which made you say, "Wow, I used to think like this now, but this looks very interesting."

When he died, I took every single one of his classes and downloaded them, including some of his khutbah's and Q&As. I plan to go over them again. By the way, he had a tremendous respect for Imam Malik. I remember him saying that it is by universal consensus that he is the tops in fiqh and tops in hadith. He said, "This is by consensus." I never forgot that part. Huge respect. Actually, he says a lot of things that agree with Imam Malik.

An Andalusia of Heart and Soul

February 17, 2017, Alianza Islamica

By Yahya Figueroa Abdul-Latif

Director, Alianza Islamica

Part 2 of 3

What was Andalusia? Islam has come full circle in the West today. Daily we hear of various horrible events and atrocities unfairly attributed to the noble Quran and Blessed Prophet (PBUH). Insane terrorists, the Islamophobic media, and politicians share the same distorted propaganda against our faith. A full range of bad, shocking, and horrible images are paraded daily. Yet against this background, Islam still grows, and its brilliance of faith continues to win people amazingly. Just as in the origin of Islam, a tiny, obscure circle of people has grown into a formidable community throughout the West. This faith-nation encompasses many ethnic and racial groups. All are haunted by the hideous specter of radical madmen destroying much of the Muslim homeland.

We Spanish speaking and cultural Latino Muslims have also been thrown into this whirlwind and are, with Allah's grace, expanding rapidly.

We are confronted with the most burning issue: the reality of our direction and choice for our future. Will we jump on the bandwagon of the current troubled Islamic mode, poorly translated from one language and culture onto another? Or will we insist that our path is Andalusian, which is neither East nor West, but a spiritual reality?

In the first scenario, a few of our brightest will go to Muslim lands, master the formal structure of prayers and

44

religious formalities, and bring back the current ideals and aspirations of Arabia, Pakistan, or wherever they may happen to go.

But what Alianza Islamica of Spanish Harlem has always sought to do was to identify and revive the spirit of Old Andalusia. This land brought forth many of the leading religious and secular giants of Islam and the entire world. Or will we emulate the same worn-out failed models throughout the troubled Muslim world uncritically, mechanically, and then expect that it can achieve something for our people other than the misery that surrounds so much of the Muslim world today. I am arguing, pleading, that we exert ourselves to be true descendants of Andalusia and discover the marvels of that time and place that was a beacon of faith, learning, genuine science, tolerance, and enlightenment. It was Andalusia that opened the modern world to the classics of antiquity by way of Arabic translations from Greek, and eventually inspired the founding of the New World itself. If Spanish Islam in the West has any authentic future, it can only be by recovering its Andalusian heritage and building upon that. The other sad alternative is to march blindly to the tunes of fanatics, and the spiritually deaf and dumb whose final message seems to be homicidal suicides and ancient blood cults.

I boldly hope that we may even provide future generations in traditional Muslim homelands and minorities in Europe a message of hope and a path to a liberating future. This road to New Andalusia is not simple, nor can it be the project of a few self-obsessed fame seekers.

We must not forget the inherent contradiction of that land, which was a significant factor in its decline—the failure to achieve harmony among the competing ethnic and racial groups that made up our homeland. The same dynamic we witness here today: some racial, ethnic groups dominate all the others with no concern for society's well-being. In time those conflicts lead to the total collapse of Muslim culture and the retaking of Andalusia by non-Muslims who did not maintain the tolerant vision for which Andalusia was famous.

Will our Spanish Islam be a vision, a dream of the highest form of spirituality and social order, or merely a faulty translation from one failed society to another when we are, as a minority, already the most vulnerable? A choice is ahead of us: a living, vibrant future, or a sad repetition of a failed vision.

A few spiritual gems from Andalusian Spirituality:

'Beware of fame-seekers who use religion for power and wealth—sellers of religion. Their real desire is to be on stage in front of the crowd, exploiting them for money, women, and praise of people.

Again, from the Andalusian Classics:

This is a quote of the Holy Prophet (PBUH): 'Actions are according to intentions, and everyone will get what was intended. Whoever migrates with an intention for Allah and His messenger, the migration will be for the sake of Allah and his Messenger. And whoever migrates for worldly gain or to marry a woman, then his migration will be for the sake of whatever he migrated for.'

You don't always have to be talking to be heard.

You don't always have to be center stage to be seen.

A Radio Interview, 1991, Part 1

Speaker 1:

Now, stay tuned for Hispanic New York with Alda Sholianos.

Alda Sholianos:

Good morning. My name is Alda Sholianos. Welcome to another edition of Hispanic New York, and a very interesting show I have for you today. Incidentally, I've had some of the same people as I've had before, but I have one gentleman here, and I didn't make a very great effort for him to be here, but I wanted him, and he's here. And he's going to explain some of the things that confuse a lot of us about Islam and so on. His name is Ocasio. Yes, that's right, his name is Spanish, but then we have a young lady who is also Hispanic in name, she is a Maryam Figueroa Vasquez. She's here again. And then of course, we have Shafqat Hussain, and he's here with us. We will have an interesting show, take my word, a very interesting show. Good morning.

Rahim Ocasio:

Good morning

Shafqat Hussain:

Good morning.

Maryam Figueroa Vasquez:

Good morning.

Alda Sholianos:

Sometimes, you get a lot of response to the shows, and sometimes you wonder why people don't seem to be

47

reacting. Well, people have been reacting to some of the last shows you did, and you've had the same experience, I think?

Shafqat Hussain:

Yes.

Alda Sholianos:

What do people think about the show, those who have heard it? How do they react? What impression did you get that they get the show?

Shafqat Hussain:

I have an impression from the people, they have called me, there was real interest in the show. They want to know what Islam means. They want to hear about Muslims, whatever we've been talking about. They finally find they're very interesting shows, and I'm here to tell them again, that Islam is peace and the religion of 1400 years ago, given by prophet Mohammad.

Alda Sholianos:

Islam means peace.

Shafqat Hussain:

Peace.

Alda Sholianos:

And Islam, as a religion, is about 1400 years, as far as you know.

Shafqat Hussain:

As far as we know, yes.

Alda Sholianos:

One thousand four hundred years old, and you think it's due for another 1400 years.

Shafqat Hussain:

It will go to the end.

Alda Sholianos:

Why?

Shafqat Hussain:

Because that's the religion of the beginning and the end.

Alda Sholianos:

It's a religion that goes from beginning to end, but in the end, we can never tell when the end will be.

Shafqat Hussain:

When the end comes.

Alda Sholianos:

It may just go on and on as long as there are humans.

Shafqat Hussain:

Right, but Christians believe there is a Day of Judgment. That's the day, it will all end when we're going to have a Day of Judgment in front of God.

Alda Sholianos:

But we don't see that in the immediate future.

Shafqat Hussain:

Maybe, you never know. It can be today too.

Alda Sholianos:

And it could be a lot further away.

Shafqat Hussain:

Far away, yes.

Alda Sholianos:

I see. In other ways, Islam, it's not much different than Christianity.

Shafqat Hussain:

Not that much. The basic point is that all the prophets came from the same God. They're all messengers of God, and they brought the same message to the people of God.

Alda Sholianos:

I see.

Shafqat Hussain:

We believe, prophet Mohammed is the last prophet of God, and we emphasize that he has given the last word of God to the people of God to believe that he is the last and the only prophet at this time.

Alda Sholianos:

I see. All right, now let me ask something, Rahim.

Rahim Ocasio:

Rahim.

Alda Sholianos:

What does Rahim mean?

Rahim Ocasio:

Rahim means merciful one.

Alda Sholianos:

Merciful one. I thought there was some meaning to the Rahim, and you're Ocasio.

Rahim Ocasio:

Ocasio.

Alda Sholianos:

You know, I know a couple of Ocasios. I think I know some of your people, but that's not what we talk about. Rahim Ocasio, why did you embrace Muslim as a religion?

Rahim Ocasio:

Because of the overall concept, but I wanted to elaborate on something that he was saying.

Alda Sholianos:

That's fine.

Rahim Ocasio:

On a point, see, it's the concept of Islam. Islam doesn't just mean peace. That's one of its secondary meanings. It actually means submission. We think that the entire universe is submitting to an irresistible force.

Alda Sholianos:

Power.

Rahim Ocasio:

Divine being. The word Islam is tied to our concept of the unity of God. We believe that everything is in a state of Islam. In a sense, everything is Muslim because Muslim means one who submits. We are submitting, and the entire universe is submitting because every atom is functioning according to its very nature. The entire universe, the galaxies, the stars, supernovas are all following inexorably a law, a plan that was articulated and designed by one Supreme Creator. Inherent in the concept of Islam is the concept of the unity of the Creator. We believe that everyone is a Muslim. We believe that is the very nature of the universe in the sense that all must submit to its Creator and cannot deviate from that. In a sense, we were born Muslim.

Alda Sholianos:

Rahim, let me ask you something then. If Islam is that universal force you're talking about, a oneness about it, how would you conceive of other religions, like Christianity.

Rahim Ocasio:

Any way of life that doesn't conform to the very nature of human beings. In other words, what was the purpose of sending prophets? The purpose of sending prophets was the Creator attempting to communicate to man what they cannot instinctively follow. You will see with your eyes. You will hear through your ears. You can't see through your nose nor smell with your eyes.

Alda Sholianos:

Each sense has a designed purpose.

Rahim Ocasio:

Each has a designed purpose. However, it was part of the plan that there was a certain aspect of your life, your social, moral, the things which pertain to man as a social animal, which were not going to be programmed in him. He's not like an ant who instinctively knows how to build a nest or a bee who knows how to build a hive. He was going to have to, as an act of faith, accept that willingly to complete his submission, in order to become a Muslim in its totality. A prophet would come with a particular message, and it would be up to him whether to accept or reject, to complete his submission in the affairs of which he has no instinctive way to follow, in which he had to be instructed, or he can reject it.

Alda Sholianos:

Boy, I won't say I understand all of it, but I'll do the best I can. It's fantastic the way you explain things. We have with us again, Maryam.

Maryam Figueroa Vasquez:

Maryam.

Alda Sholianos:

Maryam Figueroa Vasquez. One of the things I wanted to make a remark on is that, I've been doing these shows or dealing with the question of Islam and all that for almost five weeks now, because my audience, some of the people that listens to it asked me to do some more, so I just keep on doing it. It never occurred to me that there'd be so many Hispanics who are Muslims. Why are they? Why are there so many Hispanic Muslims?

Maryam Figueroa Vasquez:

I think it's because there is a conscious awakening among Hispanics, especially Puerto Ricans, to say that they are getting true knowledge and true history of the fact that Spain was under Muslim rule for 900 years before Christianity.

Alda Sholianos:

That's true, yes.

Maryam Figueroa Vasquez:

It has been denied to us. We did not have that much knowledge for us to realize that our true faith and our true way inherently should be Islam, the Muslim faith, because we did not have that knowledge. It was suppressed. A lot of people do not know that. If you go to the Island of Puerto Rico, everything is Christian, and everything is Catholic. That was the first religion that was brought onto that island.

Alda Sholianos:

And to Puerto Rico.

Maryam Figueroa Vasquez:

No one ever said that Spain was under Muslim rule before Christianity came in. Not only that, if you look at the culture and the ways and the mannerisms and the adab, the etiquette of any Latino culture, it is totally Muslim-like, the way the women behave and the way the men behave.

Alda Sholianos:

One can see the way Latino women behave and realize it's not really Spanish, is it? That must be Muslim. We accepted as a matter of course; we don't argue with it. We say,

"That's strange. Why do you say that? Oh, never mind."
Because we know we, we understand it.

Rahim Ocasio:

It's even deeper than that. Our whole concept of being a Latino is actually affected by Islam. There are only two nations on the planet earth that define themselves by religion and by language.

Alda Sholianos:

What countries are those?

Rahim Ocasio:

Those are the Arabs who are multiethnic. There's black and white, all kinds of Arabs, even Berbers in North Africa. Yet, because they adopted the language, as Islam spread, and the religion, they considered themselves Arabs. Those people were in Spain for seven or eight centuries. When they left...

Alda Sholianos:

or driven out.

Rahim Ocasio:

When the Spaniards began to embark on their conquest of the new world, they brought a totally new concept. It wasn't new, but it was new to the new world, but it had its parallel. People became Latinos based on what, race?

Alda Sholianos:

No.

Rahim Ocasio:

No. On language, and at that time, the Roman Catholic religion. The proselytizing of the Catholics, as well as the imparting of their language, created Latinos. Now you have two parallel peoples: Muslim Arab culture that identified themselves by language and religion, and another culture, which, though it expelled the Muslims, began to mimic and parallel what they picked up over those years and created an entirely new people based on the same concept, one that's unique in the world. Only in those two instances does that exist.

Alda Sholianos:

Is that correct?

Maryam Figueroa Vasquez:

Yes, I would have to totally agree with my brother.

Alda Sholianos:

You totally agree with that point of view. I'm not being converted, but some of the things you say and the way you say them, I can identify with some. For instance, there are times one says, "You're not behaving like a Latino." Then you say, he must be something else. It doesn't make sense for him not to behave like a Latino. Any kind of way he acts, talks, or behaves becomes Latino, and then it could be Muslim, who knows? What do you think?

Maryam Figueroa Vasquez:

It depends on what you define as a behavior of a Latino person.

Alda Sholianos:

Let's just stick with Muslim, please.

Maryam Figueroa Vasquez:

Or a Muslim. I think by nature, the Latino men have been raised to be providers and maintainers of their wives, and their family as a whole, especially the women, protective of women. And not just do I think, but I know that women are raised to be obedient and to be kind of subservient. I don't mean that to be in a fearful way, but with a kind of kindness to their husband due to the fact that they respect the fact that their husbands are their protectors.

Alda Sholianos:

Do you find a different number of women in other countries, for instance in England, the English woman's the same?

Maryam Figueroa Vasquez:

Yes, but I think there's a big difference in that situation due to the fact that because we are aware of the fact that our husbands are protectors, there is a misconception, I think the subservient part of it, where the public might think that we are in a lesser realm of things.

Alda Sholianos:

Because you're women.

Maryam Figueroa Vasquez:

Right, because we're women. We are equal. We have the freedom to pray, as men have the freedom to pray. We have the freedom to do many things, if we ask permission of our husbands, which is reasoning. If you don't ask permission from your husband, then how can he be your protector? If he's to be your protector, he should know where you are.

Alda Sholianos:

Where you're going and the things you do.

Maryam Figueroa Vasquez:

Right.

Alda Sholianos:

Yes.

Shafqat Hussain:

The interesting point is in the United States, there are a lot of people who are converting to Islam. For example, there are whites and blacks and Latinos that were Christian before and some other religion.

Alda Sholianos:

You see a lot of people converting to Islam, regardless of their racial background.

Shafqat Hussain:

Racial background and ethnic background or their moral background.

Alda Sholianos:

Why is that? Why are people converting so much to Islam?

Shafqat Hussain:

They finally find out that this is the way of life. This is the true way of life. They have seen the Muslim people, how they think.

Alda Sholianos:

Do you think the recent things happening, for instance, dealing with Eastern Europe, will create that?

Shafqat Hussain:

That is happening in Eastern Europe, as well as in Russia.

Alda Sholianos:

And now the...

Shafqat Hussain:

Germany and everywhere.

Alda Sholianos:

I would like to keep on talking with you a lot, but I must bring this part of our discussion to a close. My thanks to you, Mr. Hussain, Ms. Figueroa Vasquez, Mr. Rahim Ocasio.

Rahim Ocasio:

Rahim Ocasio.

Alda Sholianos:

Rahim Ocasio. See you again. I'm Alda Sholianos. Thank you for listening. Good morning.

A Radio Interview, 1991, Part 2

Announcer:

Now stay tuned for Hispanic New York with Alda Sholianos.

Alda Sholianos:

Good morning. I'm Alda Sholianos. Here I am again. And this is the last of the programs, for a while anyway, that we'll be doing with my Hispanic friends. We'll be doing more shows, I can assure you because the interest in these shows has been really fabulous. I'm very surprised. People have shown interest and have called and spoken to some of the people who have been on the shows, and we think we'll do it again. We'll keep on doing another series anyway.

My guest today is Mr. Hudson Clifton James, Hudson Clifton James. And then we have Ms. Maryam.

Maryam Figueroa Vasquez:

Figueroa Vasquez.

Alda Sholianos:

Figueroa Vasquez. And we have Mr... How do you pronounce the first name?

Rahim Ocasio:

Rahim.

Alda Sholianos:

Rahim Ocasio. So now we have a variety of racial groups in the program this morning. I said that to perhaps emphasize the fact that this show deals with different people, different kinds of people, and perhaps different circumstances, and it's interesting, very interesting. Good morning.

Rahim Ocasio:

Good morning.

Maryam Figueroa Vasquez:

Good morning.

Alda Sholianos:

I could do this whole show myself just talking, so I'd better turn it over to you, right? What made you become a Muslim person?

Hudson Clifton James:

What really made me become a Muslim today? Talking with brothers, the brother who is sitting on my right and the brother who is over there. For the longest while-

Alda Sholianos:

Well, the brothers who are over there are the people who are going to be on the show. It's just people he knows who's in the studio with me.

Hudson Clifton James:

Okay. Fine. Yes. I felt I got a spirit to enlighten me more in the teaching of the Muslims that I am so satisfied with, that I felt today was the day that I should become a member. And here I am.

Alda Sholianos:

So, this has been your first day as a Muslim?

Hudson Clifton James:

Yes.

Alda Sholianos:

I was going to ask; how do you feel about it?

Hudson Clifton James:

Oh, I'm feeling proud. I'm feeling great to be. But that will enlighten me more in the spiritual world, to understand and to share among the other-

Alda Sholianos:

He's using expressions that I don't understand, but I hope my listeners have a better understanding of it as time goes on, I guess. That was Mr. Hudson Clifton James. He just became a Muslim today.

Hudson Clifton James:

Yes.

Alda Sholianos:

And he's explaining to us how it came about that, of all the days in the year, today was the day. Yes, what was it? What was it? What's happened?

Hudson Clifton James:

Well, why not? I am now occupying an office in the area where the Muslims have their conferences. And by talking in the spiritual world, I felt to put more strength into what I'm doing. I felt today was the day of being a member.

Alda Sholianos:

And you're proud of it?

Hudson Clifton James:

Yes.

Alda Sholianos:

Do you get a certain satisfaction?

Hudson Clifton James:

Oh, yes.

Alda Sholianos:

Mr. James gives the impression of being happy about something.

Rahim Ocasio:

First, congratulations. Mabrook, mabrook. That's the Arabic word for congratulations.

Alda Sholianos:

What is it?

Rahim Ocasio:

Mabrook.

Alda Sholianos:

Okay. Now you're Hispanic?

Rahim Ocasio:

Puertorriqueno.

Alda Sholianos:

Puertorriqueno. And you're also a Muslim?

Rahim Ocasio:

Yes.

Alda Sholianos:

How long?

Rahim Ocasio:

Let's see. I took shahada, shahada means when I became a Muslim, on March 10, 1973.

Alda Sholianos:

That's a long time.

Rahim Ocasio:

About 18 years. I was 19 years old when I did it.

Alda Sholianos:

Other members of your family?

Rahim Ocasio:

My brother and my mother.

Alda Sholianos:

Are Muslims?

Rahim Ocasio:

Yes.

Alda Sholianos:

Okay. Do you get any particular satisfaction out of it?

Rahim Ocasio:

A tremendous amount of satisfaction. If you really feel that you have the correct way of life, you have something to offer. And if you're really sincere, you want to impart something that's of benefit to others, also. And when you see others partaking of it and benefiting also, it gives you a great sense of satisfaction.

Alda Sholianos:

That's kind of talking over my head a little bit. Could you be a little more specific?

Rahim Ocasio:

See when you're not practicing Islam, there are a lot of un-Islamic things that occur within a family, alcoholism, all manner of foolish behavior, things that we consider deviant behavior, against the Qur'an and against the commandments of the Creator. And when you see people divest themselves of all these ill manners, deviant modes of thinking or acting, and see the benefit of their flowering, of their spiritual progression, of their personality being developed, their character being improved, and their life is set in order, it can only bring a great sense of satisfaction, especially if it's a family member.

Alda Sholianos:

I see. You keep nodding your head as he was speaking, as Mr. Ocasio was speaking. Do you feel the same way he does?

Hudson Clifton James:

Oh, yes. Yes, definitely.

Alda Sholianos:

That some sort of an inspiration or it happens because of something must have appeared in their life when this must happen? What is it?

Hudson Clifton James:

As I mentioned, what he has said, I support it 100%. Well put together. It feels like it's a new creation in you.

Alda Sholianos:

Now listen, I'm not trying to convert anybody out there, and I'm not trying to convert my guests, but I really would like for them to understand that you do get a sense of something. The studio is electrified. A lot of little things are happening here. Let me go now to a young lady, Maryam Figueroa Vasquez. How do you feel about it? How long have you been a Muslim?

Maryam Figueroa Vasquez:

It's no coincidence, but inshallah, that means if Allah wills it, tomorrow will be a year for me that I reverted to being Muslim. And I'd like to take the time to congratulate the brother here...

Alda Sholianos:

You are congratulated.

Maryam Figueroa Vasquez:

... For embracing Islam, for reaching out for his salvation, for giving himself the opportunity to know the truth, and to do the biggest thing or the most essential thing that a Muslim should do for another Muslim is to spread the word on. I got a great sense of feeling when my brother Rahim was talking about the life that we lived un-Islamically. And when you become a Muslim, you strive to do the righteous things. And the joy that I share for Mr. Hudson is, there is a hadith, there is a saying that Prophet, peace be upon him. And that's what you should want for your brother, what you want for yourself. And the joy that I feel and the ability to strive to correct and to try to live the life of a Muslim woman, there are no words to describe it.

Alda Sholianos:

In other words, does it give you a great deal of satisfaction?

Maryam Figueroa Vasquez:

Absolutely. A completeness. It's like all of a sudden, I feel that Allah has given me a purpose in this life and that's to try and strive.

Alda Sholianos:

Allah means God?

Maryam Figueroa Vasquez:

Allah is God.

Alda Sholianos:

Is God. I see.

Maryam Figueroa Vasquez:

Well, Allah is Allah. Because I said before on the show, there are gods and then there is Allah. Allah stands alone.

Rahim Ocasio:

You must understand that what the West doesn't understand is that we use the terminology of the Qur'an or what the Prophet used, and it creates totally different concepts. The word religion is not the same as it is in Islamic terminology. Din means life.

Alda Sholianos:

Explain it. How the religion is not the same as it is Islam.

Rahim Ocasio:

No, religion has to do a lot with personal belief in rituals in the Western concept. That's why you can talk about separation of church and state. In Islam, that's of course impossible because in Islam, religion is not translated properly. It's Din. Din means lifestyle, system of life.

Alda Sholianos:

A way to live?

Rahim Ocasio:

And that means it covers every aspect, economic, political, juridical. Every single aspect of life is covered comprehensively. So, we have our own morals, political laws, social laws, jurisprudence, economic laws. Everything is totally included in the Islamic concept. So, in the sense of a separation between church and state, we don't have a church. You see, it's-

Alda Sholianos:

You don't have the status of church?

Rahim Ocasio:

No, there's no church. We don't have a priesthood. There's no clerical class. That's something which in the West, they misrepresent. They think we have clerics. We have no clerics. I've been able to perform marriages. Anybody can and other things of that nature.

Alda Sholianos:

How do you feel about it, Ms. Vasquez?

Maryam Figueroa Vasquez:

I feel that it brings.

Alda Sholianos:

I mean, in terms of your becoming a Muslim.

Maryam Figueroa Vasquez:

How do I feel in terms of me becoming Muslim? I feel that I finally have the truth. But I feel something deeper than that, in that I feel a great freedom.

Alda Sholianos:

Freedom from what?

Maryam Figueroa Vasquez:

Freedom from my oppression because I felt that I had an oppression. I felt that I had to live a life the way everybody told me that I needed to live a life.

Alda Sholianos:

I see, you felt that you were-

Maryam Figueroa Vasquez:

I felt that I needed to behave the way everybody else was behaving.

Alda Sholianos:

I see.

Maryam Figueroa Vasquez:

I felt that I needed to dress, act, to live a social life, the way everybody else in this world had to tell me.

Alda Sholianos:

And being a Muslim, you don't have to do that? You can do what you...

Maryam Figueroa Vasquez:

Being a Muslim, you strive to live the life according to His rules and regulations. And He gives you a description of how to live. So, you don't live for others. You live to please and to be subservient to Allah.

Alda Sholianos:

I see. Now you see, Mr. James, Hudson Clifton James.

Hudson Clifton James:

Yes.

Alda Sholianos:

You've really taken on a big job here, haven't you?

Hudson Clifton James:

Well, yes. I have to say that, to strengthen what I intend to do. See, in the religious faith, you must know thyself, which today I added on another link, that I could see further in life.

Alda Sholianos:

Now let me ask something. Suppose I were to ask you, I would just say to you, say now to all these people listening to you on the radio that you are a Muslim and that you're inviting them to be a Muslim. What could you say to them that will convince them?

Hudson Clifton James:

Well, I am not here to convince anyone. Freely they have to come. All I want to tell them if they want to live a righteous life, is to join up with the Muslims. Read about them. Listen, and then they will come to it themselves.

Alda Sholianos:

How do you feel about that?

Rahim Ocasio:

Well, Allah says that sincerity will come to those who are truly sincere. Because no one will actively seek the Creator and God will deprive them of the knowledge of His existence and the true way of life. If a person sincerely seeks guidance, he will be given that guidance.

Alda Sholianos:

Do you think, Maryam, the same way they feel about it?

Maryam Figueroa Vasquez:

Absolutely.

Alda Sholianos:

Then your decisions are not your decisions. It's someone else's or it's God's?

Maryam Figueroa Vasquez:

That's right. Nothing moves, but before the power of Allah.

Rahim Ocasio:

No, we do make our own decisions.

Maryam Figueroa Vasquez:

Yes, we do because we have free will. Allah gave us the free will to make choices. And we can either choose to go on the right path or go on the wrong path.

Alda Sholianos:

Well, let me ask you something. Suppose you were to go to a Roman Catholic church. I'm Catholic, and I said, "Would you come with me to church Sunday," or whatever. Could you go with me and still be a Muslim?

Rahim Ocasio:

I mean, if we're doing that as a courtesy, not in the sense of partaking in the rituals itself, maybe as an observer, there is nothing wrong with that. Of course, if we were partaking in the rituals, you would see there's a clear contradiction there. But there's still no problem. We have high respect for Christians and Jews. We consider them People of the Book because they have been given a prior tradition of prophethood and divine literature, and we respect that. And that's well respected in Islamic tradition.

Alda Sholianos:

Do you feel the same way?

Maryam Figueroa Vasquez:

Absolutely.

Alda Sholianos:

You said absolutely, but you must remember I don't know exactly. How do you feel about your religion, Muslim, in terms of Christianity?

Maryam Figueroa Vasquez:

Well, I was born and raised a Catholic, though that choice was made for me by my parents, and I practiced it while I was under their discipline. But I noticed that as I got older, I was practicing something because that's what I was told to do. And as the time wore on for me, I started to feel a spiritual void, and my religion of being Catholic was not fulfilling my spiritual void. Not only that, but I also saw that the Catholic religion modernized itself according to what was happening in the world, so I found it to be very hypocritical.

Alda Sholianos:

Well, that's about bringing us towards the end of this show. And it would be good to hear from you next time. How do you feel about the religion as far as the people who listen to this show are concerned? Let me know, in other words, if people hear you and how they react to you, will you? I'd be very glad to know. I'm Alda Sholianos. My thanks to our guests. Thank you for listening. Good morning.

Announcer:

You've been listening to Hispanic New York, a public affairs presentation of WOR, the talk station.

Reclaiming our Heritage

February 17, 2017, Alianza Islamica

By Yahya Abdul-Latif Figueroa

Director, Alianza Islamica

Part 3 of 3

Reclaiming heritage lends itself to the false impression of dwelling on the past. The next few lines are about the future flowing from the past. Hopefully, a reopening to a humble beginning accomplished many great starts and confronted many challenges. It now must map a way forward that can build on that past and hopefully sidestep the errors and continue to shed new light and hope for our future. Part one of this article recalled several accomplishments and sought to establish the development of Alianza. It also mentioned the challenges that ultimately led to insurmountable hurdles.

We recalled the tensions that confronted Muslims worldwide, leading ultimately to the horror of 9/11, a philosophy of despair overwhelmed with hopelessness and a vision of mass suicide. Muslims in modern times have sought ways to modernize while remaining faithful to their culture. Alianza faced the same dilemma with the added complexity of being new Muslims in the very center of the most complex modern city in the world.

From the very beginning, Alianza faced some Muslims' concern that they had segregated themselves from the broader Muslim community. We responded in two ways.

The essential message of the Quran stresses the universal brotherhood of all people. Racism, which holds that one race is superior to others, is a uniquely modern European invention that has spread havoc worldwide.

Racist ideology is as opposed to Islam as is paganism or polytheism. Indeed, we believe that racism is related to these false concepts of the deity. On the other hand, there is a healthy recognition of Andalusia's unique culture, and we believe it can navigate Muslims not only in the US but worldwide as it did for centuries.

Recall that from our long-lost homeland came the leadership of Ibn Hazm, Ibn Rushd, and Ibn Arabi. Ours was a land of grand jurists, Quran masters, philosophers, and the greatest Sufi masters of all time. Leave for the time the flight of Ibn Arabi and turn to the exceedingly sober orthodox message of Ibn Abbad of Ronda. You can glimpse the greatness of our past, which must not be silenced by the ignorance and fanatics of our post-colonial setting.

Andalusia is a heritage we must grasp with courage and leave the crippled version of Islam that has reduced the Muslim world to shambles in so many places. We learn that much of the destruction of Andalusia came about through racial and ethnic conflict. The beauty of old Spain did not pay full attention to peasants and the poor, and in time financial instability eroded the fabric of life. These are dangers that we face as well today. We face the destruction of the basics of faith that the entire Andalusian world shared – firm belief in monotheism, prophethood, life after death, and basic morality. These are no longer held as certainties.

A few forward-looking suggestions. An all-out effort to explore the precious treasures of Andalusian spirituality and thought. This endeavor will require experts in all of

Andalusian learning's traditional branches—not least the Arabic treasures, which number among the vastest among Arabic writings. A commitment to forging a political-cultural vision for our people based on past wisdom is required. Yet, it must be fully able to engage and challenge the many false trends and philosophies among Muslims and others. Finally, this commitment must tackle the terrible social and economic instability, which most of our people share with much of the Third World.

At City Lore in Manhattan

Founded in 1986, City Lore is New York City's center for urban folk culture. Its mission is to foster New York City — and America's — living cultural heritage through education and public programs in service of cultural equity and social justice. This speech was presented on May 13, 2017.

Molly Garfinkel:

Greetings Facebook friends near and far. Thank you so much for joining us tonight. Live from New York, it's Saturday night at City Lore, first and first in the historic lower East Side. I'm Molly Garfinkel, director of Place Matters, and we are so glad that you're here to join us for this evening's program "Stories from the Intersection of Latinx and Muslim." And here is Sahar Muradi, our director of poetry programs introducing the program.

Sahar Muradi:

Welcome folks. I'd like to introduce our first speaker, Brother Rahim Ocasio, he's a graduate of Fordham University and converted to Islam 44 years ago. He was a Guidance Council member for the Washington D.C. Branch of the Islamic Party of North America. He was a copy editor and a contributing editor for The Message, one of the nation's leading Islamic magazines. You can grab the current issue in the back. He also has a featured article in it. Brother Rahim has lectured on Islam at Boricua College, NYU, Cooper Union, and Rutgers. He's also lectured on the legacy of Islamic Spain at Baruch College, New York City College of Technology, Northeastern University in Chicago, and America's Islamic Heritage Museum in Washington, D.C.

Rahim is co-founder of Alianza Islamica, the first Islamic organization to serve the needs of the Latino community in the United States. Please welcome Brother Rahim.

Rahim Ocasio:

You don't mind if I sit. Right? I'd like to have a little bit of informality. I have a daunting task. I have to condense four decades into 15 minutes. I accepted Islam 44 years ago, and I'll be 64 in a few weeks. In those days, Islam in the Latino community was virtually nonexistent. I believe I was one of the first 10 Latino Muslims ever in the city. I think I knew about three or four before me. So, I know I'm within the top 10 somewhere. There weren't a lot of them.

When Islam was introduced to Latinos, it was through Afro-Americans. Many of them came through the Nation of Islam. Many I would call crypto Latinos because if you went to a masjid in those days and you saw a Boricua and went up to him and said "Oye, como estas, hermano?" They would say in a whisper "You can't speak Spanish here. "They had this thing about wanting to meld into some kind of Afro-American version of what Islam was supposed to be about, which was really hard on us.

The story of Alianza Islamica and the movement arose from four teenagers. I was one of them. They were Johnny Figueroa, Freddy Gonzales, Mark Ortiz, and me. At that time, Ray Ocasio. We were involved in the tumult of the 60s and 70s, a very militant period. A period when there was a lot of foment in society. The place was convulsive. There was the influence of, among others, the Black Panther Party, the Student and Nonviolent Coordinating Committee, and, of course, what influenced us most, the Young Lords Party.

The Young Lords party was militant, socially activist, and against oppression, and police abuse. We were raised in this milieu. The Islam we understood and accepted is not the perverted one that exists today in my view. It was oriented towards social activism. It was very militant. We saw a smooth transition between becoming Muslim and continuing the same kind of militant social activism that we were engaged in before with the Young Lords Party. We didn't see any difference in it, and we just continued in that vein. That's what led me to join the Islamic Party in North America in Washington, D.C., because we saw that as an expression of the same kind of social activism, the same type of fight against oppression and injustice that we were waging before.

Except, now we were doing it "Islamically," and we thought we were doing it in a much more moral, in a much more substantial, much more substantive way. That's what attracted people. If you were to take a cross-section of people that became Muslim at that time, many were right off university campuses. They were people who were involved in the Black Panther Party or SNCC. These were the people that became Muslim, and this is how they understood Islam. It was just a natural progression.

Latinos had to deal with coming into our new Islamic identity, trying to forge an Islamic identity. That was hard in those days because people couldn't relate to the fact that Latino and Muslims coincided. I mean, they would actually say, "You can't possibly be a Muslim because you're Puerto Rican," which is really weird.

In other words, Puerto Rican and Muslims somehow didn't match. With Afro-Americans, we had a little bit of a problem, too, though not in the same way. Because the

Black Power movement so influenced them, and the Nation of Islam, they had a lot of trouble dealing with light-skinned Puerto Ricans. They treated us like whites. That was a problem. We had spent our teenage years organizing rent strikes, demonstrating, taking over university campuses, fighting for the independence of Puerto Rico, and now we were in totally unchartered waters.

Where did we fit in here? Once at a mosque, an Afro-American came over to us while we were speaking Spanish and said "You can't speak Spanish in the mosque. You can't do that here." I countered, "Would you have told that Pakistani over there that he couldn't speak Urdu?" Of course, he would have said no. That's the point. We're not to be under anybody's thumb. I mean, everybody's looking for a whipping boy. But we had to take a stance because we weren't going to be anybody's whipping boy. Still, there was a problem with accepting us.

We tried to put together a Spanish masjid. We got together, Colombianos, Dominicanos, Panamenos, Brasilenos, Puertorriquenos in an attempt to put together a Spanish masjid. The reaction of the Muslim community at the time was really interesting. They thought we were dividing the community, that we shouldn't attempt to do this and there was a smear campaign. All kinds of things happened. We were even evicted from our meeting place. People took that very, very strongly for some reason.

In those days, we were not considered much of anything. Right now, Latino Muslims are the Muslim group du jour; now there are conferences and articles, et cetera. Not then. I feel I can express it better in little snippets, in anecdotes.

Ibrahim Gonzalez, a co-founder of Alianza Islamica, went to Indiana in the '80s to work for ISNA, the Islamic Society of North America at the time, we didn't have one single Spanish brochure, not one single anything in the United States. He took a brochure and translated it. It was a very popular one called "Islam at a Glance". He translated it to "Islam A Un Vistazo." Those days were pre-computer. So, you had to make plates. He presented it to ISNA at their headquarters.

"Here, all you have to do is print it.

No.

I've laid out the work for you."

"No".

He presented it again, and again, and they refused to do it. Not one single brochure. He was furious. He returned to New York, and he said, "Look, we got to do something to change this totally." He came up with a brilliant idea. "You know what? We're going to pick a venue, a high-profile venue." We picked El Museo del Barrio on Fifth Avenue. The event was called "Reclamando Nuestra Herencia Islamica, Reclaiming our Islamic Heritage."

Speaker 4:

There are more seats up here, folks.

Rahim Ocasio:

I must point out the director of Alianza Islamica just walked in. This is a big surprise. It was he and I who established Alianza Islamica.

Anyway, we staged this event. It was a big success. We had our mothers, sisters, and daughters coming, creating Latin food and everything, and it was a big success. After that, the phones were ringing off the hook. Now, all of a sudden, we were on the map, and everybody wanted us to attend conferences. Of course, the way I looked at it, they were just looking for something a little juicy to put on their annual reports when asking for overseas funding. I saw what they were doing. So, I wouldn't say we told them to go to hell, but it was like that. We saw a need to create something that was our own. So how much time do I have?

Sahar Muradi:

You're good. You have 10 minutes.

Rahim Ocasio:

10 minutes? Oh, good.

Sahar Muradi:

Actually, 8.

Rahim Ocasio:

After that experience, we were going to have to do something that related to us in our neighborhoods, not relying on anyone else. Yahya and I had long talked about a dream that we had of having a center smack dab in the area where we were raised. It was to be an unassuming, organic, part of the neighborhood where people could come in and listen to the message of Islam and where we would also be able to provide services.

We finally were able to do that, but it came from the most unlikely of sources. Yahya has been working for years with people who had substance abuse problems and was able to gather many people around him. They converted to Islam and were meeting at his duplex on 12th Street, on park benches, and retreats in the Poconos. They started coming to a class that I was giving. The numbers were so large that all the seats and available floor space were taken. These were people fresh out of rehab. They became the core of Alianza Islamica. They went on to create GED programs and ESL programs. We were the first to ritually wash the bodies of Muslims who had died of AIDS because the reaction of established mosques in those days was positively medieval. They thought it was the wrath of God and didn't even want to touch them.

But Alianza and I especially have to give credit to Yahya back there. He took the lead and said, "No, we're going to wash their bodies." We're going to take it upon ourselves to have drug programs and have job programs. We're going to try to make an impact in the community and show that we're not just here. Too many Muslims are in their communities, but they make no difference. They're just masjids, just mosques. Muslim women veiled from head to toe might as well be specters floating by. They don't have any relationship with their neighborhood, to their community. This is not the Islam that I learned. This is not the Islam I understood.

The Islam I understood engaged with society, made a difference in society, and opposed racial injustice and oppression, economic, or otherwise. When you study Islam, that's the only conclusion that you could reach. I don't know how anybody else understands it any other way unless they're looking at it with a completely distorted mind.

Unfortunately, we had to offer many counseling services to Latinas, especially Puerto Rican women, because there's a tremendous predilection among Arabs to go after them, marry them, and then abuse the heck out of them.

Yahya had to deal with so many cases of these people from other cultures, marrying our woman, and abusing them, physically and emotionally. That problem exists to this day. We formed a cordon of security to make sure that our women were protected from any kind of abuse. That didn't apply to everybody, but it happened to too many. It's a big problem.

Yahya and Alianza Islamica were instrumental in dealing with people who had fallen into hard times. After converting to Islam, they needed someone to help them get their life together. In time, we've been able to establish ourselves as a legitimate Latino subgroup and one that's not necessarily anybody's whipping boy, because that was important.

The term Alianza Islamica means Islamic Alliance. The term came about because organizations try to co-opt us. We said, "You know something? You're getting a phone call, I'm getting a phone call, he's getting a phone call. We have to let them know that we're one block, we're one unit. We're not going to be your tool for your annual reports." We had to pick a name, and we picked Alianza Islamica. That was a name that sent a message. We're independent. We're not relying on you. We're doing our own thing. We were left all by ourselves in Spanish Harlem and did what we wanted. We didn't answer to any other major organization, whether immigrant or domestic. How are we doing on time?

Sahar Muradi:

Yes. I'd like to show the video now, so.

Rahim Ocasio:

Yes. My time is up.

Sahar Muradi:

You may want to say what became of Alianza and where you are today.

Rahim Ocasio:

When we moved to the Bronx, we lost our roots. It never was the same. It's interesting how, when you take a tree and plant it somewhere else, if it's not on the same fertile ground. It basically dissipated, the fire took our building, and we all got older and went in different directions. It's time for a whole new generation to step up. Because now we're all in our 60s, and we gave it our run, and we would like people to take it from here.

I don't know if that's four decades in 15 minutes? I did the best I could in that short space of time. But I'd like to show you a video here. It's a little pictorial, a little slideshow. Some pictures just to show you where Alianza was and different little things there.

Sahar Muradi:

We'll hear more from you during our question and answer. I apologize that you had to shrink so much history, and there's so much stuff untold. But we will have more from Brother Rahim in a little bit. So just play it?

Rahim Ocasio:

Yes. Just play it.

Sahar Muradi:

Okay. (Singing). Thank you so much.

Alianza Islamica and Andalusia

February 17, 2017, Alianza Islamica

By Yahya Abdul-Latif Figueroa

Director, Alianza Islamica

In these next few lines, I want to boldly assert that Alianza was truly unique as a voice of Spanish Islam and that its vision and mission must be reclaimed and built again. I want to stress that other groups today that are attempting to monopolize a Spanish Islamic message are simply copying the failed message of some Middle Eastern patterns. These groups are cut off from the brilliance of Islam's message and the genuine difference it could make in today's world. Finally, I want to recall our small community members who have left this world and have returned to their Lord.

To the best of our knowledge, Alianza was the first group of Spanish speakers to have built a small, distinct Muslim group in Harlem, NY, with the clear vision that they wanted to build upon Islam's understanding over the long centuries of Muslims in Spain. We learned as we lived and strove together as a group to bring our heritage's spiritual message to shine light upon the often very troubling conditions of life here in the US. The problematic situations we and many of our Afro-American brothers, sisters, and neighbors inherited were poverty, disease, and family dysfunction. Our Islam was one of survival and growth.

Today many of our "Muslim" groups are an elitist bunch who live among ideas, often not very good ones, yet compassion and service of others are not high on their deluded agendas. Often, they have brought from the failed

Middle East a caste approach, placing the pampered university crowd in authority for no legitimate reason other than the privilege we have afforded them. Alianza will revive a message of social relevance alongside our proud Islamic spiritual understanding. We will not adopt the failures that can only bring more of the same and even worse.

Two examples of our experiment are worth noting, each deserving a full biography. These accounts are simply an introduction to their lives. Both were active supporters and leaders in the activities of our small, beautiful community.

Amin Madera.

He was a worshiper, simple, humble, and a source of inner strength for those fortunate enough to have known him. Amin was not sophisticated or learned, yet he loved Islam and was convinced that Alianza was the place where Allah Almighty had opened the doors to Islam for him. There were many more sophisticated and better off places throughout the city of New York, yet nowhere was as appropriate to bring brother-sisterhood to him nor offered a loving environment that met his spiritual and communal needs. Amin battled a disease that he had contracted in his earlier life. Alianza provided him with the brotherhood and friendship needed to carry his burden. He passed away among these same friends who laid him to rest in Islamic fashion. Such was among his last great desires. Cheerful, hopeful, and trusting in our Glorious Lord's plan, he returned peacefully to his final home.

The second person from our circle, I must mention, was Sharif Abdul Karim, scholar and intellectual master of the old Arabic sciences, and yet at home in the world of current intellectual pursuit. Sharif was university trained and had done graduate studies at a prominent New York institution. He was one of many African-American member/supporters of our community and, for years, shared his great learning with us in many of the standard fields: tafsir, hadith, fiqh, and his favorite, spiritual culture. A giant in the world of ideas, his humility and lack of desire for recognition rivaled his brilliance. A glaring shortcoming of many of the current leaders who traffic in religion is their lust for notoriety. Sharif had stayed at the Azhar university for several years and had spent years in Mecca studying and collecting classical Arabic books. It is no exaggeration to state that at his death, he had one of the largest Arabic libraries in the country. Sharif had mastered bringing the challenging ideas and treasures of these ancient texts to a level that the simplest soul could benefit from.

Sharif and Amin are no longer here, but their legacy of profound brotherhood and spiritual greatness remains a guide for us in our commitment to revive the message of Alianza Islamica of Harlem, NY.

Latino Muslim's Perspective on Racism within the Muslim Community

This presentation took place at the ICNA-MAS Convention in 2018.

Rahim Ocasio:

I'm going to discuss a very, very important problem. And it's going to be a little bit different because when you hear these stories about discrimination, it's usually around African-Americans. Still, very little is mentioned about Latino Muslims and what they're going through. Because we're discussing here racism and Islam, and this is racism that affects not only Afro-Americans but also affects Latinos. But it's insidious because the dominant immigrant Islamic culture has treated Latinos like the flavor of the month. They're the "okay" ones. They're the "okay Muslims," so we can throw them a little bone here and there. We're not racist towards them. But they are, and it's very insidious. I don't want to put people on the spot, but how many people here have experienced racism from Muslims?

Okay.

It's very pervasive, but it's never really discussed in this kind of way. I mean, there is racism. But how many times has the community itself, the ones perpetrating the racism, have ever been confronted with it. We all feel it. But how many people are making a big deal about it?

No, you just feel it. You go home, you talk about it, get angry, and that's about it. But it's incredibly pervasive. I put all my kids through Islamic school. And a couple of years ago, my sons came to me and told me, "Papi, I hated Islamic school."

Hated it.?

That's not the reason I sent them to Islamic school, for them to come back and say they hated it. Then they told me, "For years, the Palestinian kids were bullying them, calling them names. And they got no redress from the administration." I was grateful that they remained Muslim, but that was a traumatic experience for them. And it was tough for them to hold onto their Islam, to come and tell me how much they hated going to an Islamic school. It hurt me, and it hurts me as well when my daughter gets on the subway and is approached by an immigrant Muslim and tells her, "Are you married?" "No, no, I'm not married," "But you're Muslim?" "Yeah." "Oh, you can't possibly be a Muslim. Are you Puerto Rican? Puerto Ricans cannot be Muslims. It's impossible."

And you don't know how many times that happens. Puerto Rican, Muslim, it's not supposed to go together. Because Puerto Rican means you're garbage, so you can't possibly be a Muslim. And then when he said, "Do you have a sister? And is she a virgin? Because you know how those Puerto Rican women are."

Thank God, Alhamdulillah, that I was not on the subway when that happened, because that guy would have been toast. And to show you the great disrespect, if I would have said that to him, knowing his culture, "Is your daughter a virgin?" He would have freaked out. Probably would've taken out a scimitar on me, right? These are examples of the kind of things we go through.

And it's not just confined to, say, the immigrant community, because when we first tried to bring Islam to Latinos in New York City, we would go to an Afro-American masjid and be told, "You can't even speak

Spanish here." The dynamic here is that Afro-Americans were pushed down. Now, comes another group. "That's all right. We can pick on them. Now we have somebody else that's below us." It's a natural process that people go through. That thing has to be put in check. One group feels that they're oppressed and says, "We're now going to oppress them. We have somebody else we can pick on." And it just goes on, and on, and on. These things have to be openly discussed because they're real.

We hear a lot about how African-Americans experience oppression, but when we came along, they started doing it to us, and we had to put them in check. And God forbid that another group comes along, and we start doing it. We have to continually fight against this, deal with it, and realize that it's part of our human nature. We have to resist because if we don't, it's going to be an endless chain of foolishness.

Another big problem we had in Alianza Islamic is our women's abuse. That whole subway scene with my daughter, Sultana, is indicative of what they really think of us.

We're whores. They marry Latinas sometimes for green cards, but they have no respect for them. They would see my wife dressed as a Spanish Muslim in the supermarket and would approach and ask,

"Are you Muslim?"

She replied, "Yes."

"Well, I'm married to a Muslim."

And she went on to discover he doesn't teach her any Salah, and doesn't let her touch the Qur'an, treats her like a pariah.

One day a woman explained she attended an event that she later discovered was an Eid celebration. She said, "He never even told me what this is. Never explained anything." Why? Because he was just using her. He doesn't think of her. He doesn't care. Such behavior is rampant and needs to be dealt with.

It affects Latinos. They accept Islam and immediately assume that Muslims from Muslim countries are automatically much more educated. They're "real" Muslims. One time, a group of Latinos went to see a shaykh from the Indo-Pakistani subcontinent, and one asked the question, "Was Adam black?" The shaykh replied, "Brother, how could Adam be black? All the prophets were beautiful and wise." They come back and tell me what the shaykh said." Well, I told them they'd better not accept that as gospel truth because it's absolute foolishness. And this is how pervasive it is.

As a young Muslim, I worked as a security guard and was relieving a Pakistani. I'm always curious about countries, and I was curious about his country. I asked him about the Dravidians. The Dravidians are from the Southern part of India and are darker than the people from the North. They tend to have woolier hair. He responded, "Brother, brother, black people, dirty people. Don't even talk about them", and that was that.

I was only one or two years in Islam, saying, "What the heck is going on here?" I accepted Islam. I expect to be part of a Muslim brotherhood. I believe everything I read in the Qur'an and the Hadith. Who are these jokers? After a while, it was clear to me that we have a serious problem affecting people who are converting.

Now, I'm talking specifically about Latinos. Some are getting inferiority complexes because they gravitate to certain communities and are treated a certain way. That didn't apply to me because I was a rebel from the very beginning. I wasn't buying it, but some do, and they start changing their dress, changing their mannerisms.

They don't even want to be Latino anymore. We're all over this place, but hardly anybody was at yesterday's Spanish sessions. Because now, they want to be somebody else. They want to transform. They want to be Arabs or Sudanese. They're like tablets of Alka-Seltzer. They just dissolve. It affects our community to the point that they don't even want to organize. Ask a Latino now "Do you want to do something for our people, because nobody else will do it. The reply: "That's nationalism." "That's un-Islamic."

Rahim Ocasio:

Are we all Muslims? That's a joke. We have severe problems in the community we need to deal with. And we have people who don't want to address it because they've been neutered. They don't exist. They're like... What is that stuff, Emergen-C? You drop it in, get a nice fizz, and it gives you vitamin C. Only, this is not nourishing at all. It is poison negatively affecting our communities.

Rahim Ocasio:

It's all a mind game, a mind game we must break away from. We cannot be healthy in that situation. It is a pathological situation, which urgently has to be corrected. The first cardinal sin was Iblees' refusal to bow down to

Adam. That's racism. Iblees said, "I will not bow down to someone you created from Earth because I'm created from flame." He probably thought the flame was cooler. I don't need to bow down to someone made out of dirt. And that was the first cardinal sin, the sin of racism, and the basis of man's inhumanity to man.

Because when you think that someone else is garbage or dust, you can do to them whatever you want. You can abuse them or exploit them. There must be conversations in households, open conversations. Someone has to say to an uncle or family member, "Look, I heard what you said about so-and-so, and that's wrong." We can no longer think like that." Or go into the many Muslim-run stores in Puerto Rican and Black communities and say "Papa, you can't continue to sell ham and beer, and maybe drugs under the table to these people just because you think they're dogs and make money out of it."

They wouldn't sell it to their sons or daughters, so they sell it to us? What then do they think of us?

Yahya Abdul Latif Figueroa was the director of Alianza Islamica. He was an amir in a council of amirs in New York City. He had one of his fellow council members, a Pakistani, say to him, "How do we keep our children from being corrupted by Puerto Ricans?" disrespecting him right to his face. It was absolutely ridiculous.

I went on Hajj with a brother, Muhammed. He was in Egypt with his mother. And he went through horrible experiences while there due to racism. One day, an Egyptian came up to him and asked,

 "Brother, have you been to Egypt?"

Muhammad responded, "Yes, I've been to Egypt."

"What did you think of Egypt?"

He responded, "I hated Egypt."

The Egyptian asked, "Why?"

Muhammad replied, "You know why."

That was the end of that conversation because they're very aware of how they treat us. It is no mystery.

America has never confronted its own racism. They live in a Hollywood myth. It's time for Muslims to confront their racism. This conversation needs to be brought out into the open. This is the only forum ever, I think, where a Latino has gotten up to say, "We get it too. We get the business also."

People need to go back and have serious heart-to-heart talks because this is a problem that needs correcting. I can't go into those houses and do it. It has to be addressed by open-minded people who are aware of the enormity of this situation and try to correct it themselves.

Assalamu Alaykum wa Rahmatullahi wa Barakatuhu

Back in the Driver's Seat

March 31, 2017, Alianza Islamica

By Yahya Figueroa

Intellectual fads and cultural truisms are very hard to detect. These false trends often have a grain of truth, but the final product is distorted truths and fabulous falsehoods. The larger society has, in so many ways, lost its mind morally and intellectually.

Our minority groups are usually in the rear, but here they have seemingly joined full scale adopting the lies of our time.

What happened to the most basic shared truths of the Bible and the Quran? The ideas of monotheism against paganism, both ancient and modern, and the belief in revealed truths such as the sanctity of life and the final judgment with accountability for our deeds or the revealed truth of humanity's common origin.

The condemnation of theft, cheating, immorality, and yes, shared notions of family marriage and a shared sense of normality seem outdated.

Too often, when we approach religion, we wander into hair-splitting, and the most arcane debates and the world seems to implode.

We watch helplessly as our families dissolve, and our communities are up in arms against each other.

I challenge myself today by asking what it is that is so important in my belief. How does it make a difference for me and others? Does my life have a mission, a core value that is worth calling towards, or am I just making a lot of noise?

Some of us have now spent an entire life within Western Islam. We lived humble beginnings, sweet innocent days of spiritual searching with a revolutionary desire to change the worst parts of our society. Then we watched in horror as the worst aspects of the Third World were brought here to our land.

Amazingly, we have allowed the late comers to reduce us to silence. Yes, people who came here to escape the horror of their failed lands are now the captains of this ship with the same foolish notions and collapsed plans.

Let us reclaim those days of joyous Islamic spirituality and, yes, confront the self-appointed leaders who overlook their legacy of failure.

Spiritual searching and social activism are a powerful combination whose time has come again.

Youth and Movements in America

This presentation is a comprehensive look at resistance movements from the Sixties through to the present day. It mainly focuses on the roots of resistance and how they influenced early indigenous Muslim communities. Rahim Ocasio presented it at Darul Hijra in Northern Virginia about 2013 as part of a youth program.

Rahim Ocasio:

The world of the 50's going into the 60s was undergoing a seismic world shift. Many former colonies of Britain, France, Italy, Germany were finally achieving their independence. There was optimism in the world. A new world order based on freedom, freedom from oppression, and freedom from colonialism emerged across the globe. At that time, socialism, or more accurately, Marxist Leninism, was the ideology of choice, the ideology of liberation. Many Muslim countries, such as Egypt, adopted it, believing it was the logical alternative. Here in the United States during the same period, we experienced the epic struggle for civil rights led by the Reverend Martin Luther King, its startling images engraved in our memory of people being hosed down, beaten, and attacked by dogs in the South.

By the mid-1960s, a general restlessness emerged due to the Civil Rights movement's perceived meager gains. For many, it was too slow, too deliberate, and people were getting impatient. The urban ghettos were in terrible condition.

Drugs had infested neighborhoods. In my teens, it seemed like every other person was a heroin addict. People were living in horrible squalor, much worse than anything you could imagine now. For example, where I lived, ceilings collapsed. Ceilings collapsed on my mother. Ceilings collapsed on my brother. I lived on the fifth floor of a tenement building and had to walk over "junkies" strewn on the steps covered in vomit to get to my front door. Blood-smeared walls that hadn't seen paint for years and empty glassine bags everywhere littering the floor completed the macabre decorative motif.

I went for years with no heat nor hot water. Years with no heat nor hot water. And my building was city-owned. No one cared.

Garbage pickup was so infrequent, and it led to frustrated people piling it up on the streets and setting it on fire in protest.

This anecdote will illustrate how insensitive we had become to violence. One evening, I was coming up the stairs with a basketball in my hand when I heard a shot. When I got down to the second-floor landing, I saw a young long-haired white man lying there. I looked at him and said, "Are you all right?" He said, "Yeah." I said "OK" and just walked right over him. As I walked out of the building, the cops rushed past me. The man later died, and the word on the street was that the shooter was a boy from the building next door. Nothing happened.

It was a culture of violence; it was a culture of drugs. It was a powder keg waiting to explode; not long after, it did. Major riots erupted in the streets all over the nation. In Watts, there was a great riot. In Detroit, tanks patrolled devastated neighborhoods in their attempt to control the rage of destruction.

A new militancy was born, leading to the formation of radical organizations. The most significant of these new organizations was the Black Panther Party. This socialist organization adopted all the outward rhetoric of militancy: black leather jackets, berets, and posing with shotguns. But here is a key point; they were not violent. They were there to defend the community if necessary but were more about school breakfast programs, health care, and community defense from police brutality.

They were all young people who felt they had to fight for their liberation. They had to do something. They had to be active to stop what they saw happening in their neighborhoods. They saw their communities ripped apart. They saw prostitution and police oppression. And they wanted to react in some way against it. They did so by forming organizations in service to the community.

The Young Lords Party was the Latino version of the Black Panther Party. Though it originated in Chicago, it rose to prominence in New York City. The person who first told me about it was 14 years old and already a member. When he first came to me, I was 16 and skeptical. Within a year, however, I was 17 and selling organization newspapers along with him in Harlem.

By the time I was 18, I had joined them in organizing rent strikes as part of a mass organization, a branch of the Young Lords Party called Committee to Defend the Community. We organized rent strikes against landlords seeking to abandon buildings to force them to provide services, fix the plumbing, clean the stairs, and repair the walls and ceilings. We were also interested in making sure that healthcare and daycare were available, which was unheard of at that time. Unheard of.

At the college level, Black Americans insisted on accurate information about their history and pushed for Black Studies courses. Latinos followed suit with demands for Puerto Rican studies courses. We wanted to learn about ourselves and our history to establish a sense of identity.

I participated in two campus takeovers that I remember. Let me tell you something about the spirit of youth at that time. I'd get a phone call from my friend Freddie, 15 years old. He would call me and say, "We're taking over Columbia" or "We're taking over City College." And my friend Johnny and I would say, "We're going to be right there." That night, there we were, a 15, 17, 18-years old-early warning system, the midnight watch looking out the front door windows for any signs of a police raid.

In those days, that was a genuine threat.

For example, one day, the Young Lords marched down Madison Avenue in peaceful protest of all the conditions that we were suffering in our neighborhoods.

When they got to 111th St, I saw a blue van show up. The doors flew open, and out rushed in blue helmets what we used to call in those days, the TPF, the Tactical Police Force. They were beating and clubbing everybody in sight, marchers, non-marchers. I was standing a block away on the corner of 110th Street when I saw them coming my way.

I was 17 at the time and said to myself, "I gotta get out of here." I ran into a building and remember looking back to see a kid run by and a policeman with a billy club running right after him. I had no illusions in those days about what type of country I was living in. The police in our neighborhoods were armies of occupation. They were not there to serve and protect.

There was another significant group you should be aware of. They were known as the Nation of Islam, although, in reality, they had nothing to do with Islam. They were also called the Black Muslims. They believed in a heretical version of Islam where Elijah Muhammad was the prophet of Allah (may Allah forgive me) and that God came in the person of W.D. Fard Muhammad. Aside from this heresy, they distinguished themselves by their program for self-empowerment and Black empowerment.

They believed in economic independence and coined the term, "Do for self." The Nation of Islam had restaurants, real estate, farms. They had health-food restaurants long before it became fashionable. They were the originators and popularizers of carrot cakes and bean pies so commonplace now in American cuisine. Steak and Take restaurants served the best variation of Philly Cheese Steak you could ever imagine.

In a world of drugs, prostitution, and all manner of vice, their women stood out. Their women used to dress like our Muslim women, except that they didn't bring their veils across their bodies. But they dressed impeccably and commanded respect wherever they walked. People admired them, and I liked that. There was tremendous admiration in the ghetto for people who dressed that way. The men always dressed in suits, bow ties, and, occasionally, hats. They stood out. They stopped smoking, drinking, gambling, and running around with women. They lived their version of a moral life. Though they were not true Muslims in the sense that we know, they exemplified much that was admired and respected in the community.

The Fruit of Islam was its paramilitary organization. They learned martial arts. They functioned as a unit. And they were feared, admired, and respected. Nobody would mess with a Muslim, and especially a Muslim woman. Nobody would touch them because they would have to deal with them. Could you imagine that? No one would dare speak a disrespectful word to a woman dressed in a long dress and a veil in the ghetto. Nobody. Because they knew that behind that woman, there would be an organization that they feared and respected.

Those men and women commanded respect wherever they went.

Now, look at this journey so far. From the worst kind of oppression sprung determination and action, and organizations like the Nation of Islam, SNCC, the Student Non-Violent Coordinating Committee, the Black Panther Party, and the Young Lords Party.

Remember that for the most part, these are very young people. Some of them are in their 20s. A lot of them are in their teens. Now, something eventful happens in the mid-60s. After Malcolm X's assassination, many started looking closely at his life, especially after he converted to Islam. His passing called attention to the religion that he finally adopted, the true religion of Allah. And there was an explosion of conversions. Those who converted were not only inspired by the religion of Islam, but his view of it as an answer to oppression: an activist religion of liberation, justice, and human rights.

The new converts were not accepting a religion isolated from life. They were now on a path that not only gave them salvation in the hereafter but could change their condition on earth. This mindset influenced the types of organizations these new Muslims eventually would form.

American Muslims, overwhelmingly Black Americans, established organizations geared to the empowerment of their people. They wanted to liberate them from, in their view, spiritual, mental, political, and economic slavery. And this is key to understanding the movements that came later.

There were two major organizations in the first wave; Darul Islam founded in 1962, and the American Muslim Mission, 1975.

The Darul Islam movement, headquartered in New York City, was a national organization with more chapters than any other Muslim organization. It had certain elements that were very similar to the Nation of Islam, in that it also had a paramilitary organization, the Ra'ad. Members typically wore long thobes, fatigue jackets, and boots, and drilled for combat readiness. Such action was a deterrent against potential enemies, including the Nation of Islam. Sunni Muslim groups such as Darul Islam competed with the Nation of Islam for Islamic legitimacy, and there was no longer just one Muslim group on the block.

The American Muslim Mission took a different route. After the death of Elijah Muhammad in 1975, his son Warith Deen Muhammad, did away with the teachings of his father. He desired to bring Islam into the Sunni Muslim mainstream. He changed the name of the organization to the American Muslim Mission and promoted Sunni orthodox teachings. But he still held Elijah, his heretical father, in high regard as well as W.D. Fard Muhammad, a person who claimed to be Allah. He, also, attempted to rename Afro-Americans Bilalians seeking to highlight a link to Bilal, the African sahabah.

The second wave represented an evolution of the concept of an American Islamic movement: The Islamic Party of North America. Though the Darul Islam Movement was ideologically linked to the two major movements in the Islamic world, the Ikhwanul Muslimin, and the Jamaati Islami, the Islamic Party represented something different. Officially organized in 1971, it was the first constitutionally-based Muslim-American organization in U.S. history. Their constitution was a carefully crafted amalgam of the Ikhwanul Muslimin and Jamaati Islami constitutions adapted to American conditions.

By comparison, other organizations appeared loosely based. The Islamic Party had a structure calling for national and regional administrations, clearly defined duties and term limits, and conditions and responsibilities of membership. Requirements for membership were exceedingly strict; shahadah, an oath of admission, and one-year probation. The rules and defined expectations were the same for the guidance council, the central committee, and the entire leadership structure.

The Islamic Party believed in the Islamic movement as a principle. Ideologically, they were also very much influenced by Malcolm X in the sense that Islam is supposed to be about revolutionary struggle, a struggle to break the bonds of oppression, whether economic, political, or spiritual. At the time, Islam was often referred to as an ideology, the same term that the Marxist-Leninists use. It was called revolutionary, as well. The use of these terms illustrated the mindset of the time.

Where did these brothers come from? Where did these activist brothers come from who wanted to be an American version of the Jamaat-e-Islami? Many came right off college campuses; others yet came from activist movements like the Black Panthers and the Young Lords. And some came with just the mindset and spirit for active community involvement. The Islamic Party was peppered with activists right off the campus and militant organizations, and those with a thirst for radical change. But now they thought they had the real solution, Islam, and immediately put that into practice.

Service to the community was a priority; Feed the Hungry, a food distribution program during Ramadan, soon followed. It wasn't going to be about just tarawih and prayer. The intent was to show that Muslims are out there, giving food, serving the community. We had an Oppressed Peoples Affairs Committee and dealt with other organizations that were also interested in helping people who were poor, oppressed, and underprivileged. Education was central, and we established a K through 8 for our children. Economic initiatives were represented by a restaurant, a bookstore, a bakery, and a 24-hour cab service.

The cab service ran round the clock, rotating 8-hour shifts, with all the money given to the organization in return for stipends for the drivers. This practice enabled the Party to buy "jamaat housing" for the members and their families. The spirit of sacrifice for Allah and the struggle prompted them to pool their resources to keep the organization, the machine rolling.

Remember, these were all young people. They had known oppression and decided to do something about it. They wandered in the wilderness, tried socialism and Marxism until they came to Islam with an understanding that religion is not just merely sitting in a masjid with a mishwak in your mouth and reading Qur'an.

We used to have people that would come to the mosque, and if they started hanging around for any length of time, we brought them a broom and said, "Here, that classroom needs sweeping." We may have gone overboard with it, but that's how we thought.

A frequent saying of the amir was, "There is no Islam without jamaat, and there is jamaat without leadership." We had the advantage of being an organized group, and we were optimistic. I was 22 years old and thought by the time I was 30, America would be an Islamic state. We all thought we'd be done by 30, the idealism of youth so prevalent then.

Tensions between Sunni Islam and the Nation of Islam finally reached the breaking point. As I mentioned before, Elijah Muhammad had died, and Wallace took the organization in another direction. But he was still talking in very favorable terms about his father, who claimed to be a prophet, and about Fard Muhammad. The amir of our organization ordered a front-page headline on our journal Al Islam, "Elijah and Fard must go." along with an article stating Muslims could no longer hold on to those tenets. We were sent on a three-city tour selling these papers. We were to hit New York's Times Square, Newark, and Philadelphia.

Times Square went without incident. Newark was different. We had no idea how strong the Nation of Islam was in Newark. We were harassed in the street constantly, and we could feel the tension in the air. It appeared they were looking to pick a fight. We broke for Salat. I was in the first group that made Salat. Then the second group made Salat while we stood guard. A motorcade of cars approached and parked along a line on the block across the street, very orderly. Their orderliness impressed me. The doors opened, and out they came. They formed a line, and they started walking towards us, dressed unmistakably as the Nation of Islam.

They set upon us with tire irons, claw hammers, billy clubs, and guns. We dispersed. I got my head bashed in, blood streaming down my face. I ran down to a store to call for help. The attackers beat two badly, one so severely he couldn't feel his legs. We three were put into the biggest ambulance I have ever seen. I was the one least hurt compared to them.

As we were speeding off to the hospital, one of the EMTs asked me while I lay on the gurney, "Why did they beat you up?" I didn't answer him. I went into my pocket and handed him a brochure on Islam. I remember getting blood on it. I then said, "This is why."

When we got to the hospital, some brothers from Newark came over and realized that the hospital staff was full of Nation of Islam members. They feared they would finish us off while we were in the hospital. The Islamic Party was informed, and brothers came from Washington in a motorcade to escort us out of the city.

When we got back, we were told by the amir not to tell our wives what had happened. The amir didn't want to panic the wives. I told my wife that somebody hit me with a chair or something like that. He wanted to wait because he was going to write a scathing response back. We published our response criticizing them for the attack.

Years later, I saw that person I handed the brochure to. I recognized him. He came up to me and said, "I'm the guy that you gave that brochure to while you were lying on your back. You handed me that bloody brochure." He had taken shahadah, alhamdulillah.

We were living only a few blocks away from the Nation of Islam temple. They could easily have come to my house. Yet I felt defiant, and I wasn't alone. We all were defiant, even though they threatened our lives, even though they had beaten and bloodied us. We felt we could withstand anything. Our resolve was that strong.

I went to the Islamic Party in Washington years ago, to learn about Islam, learn about the movement, learn how that type of organization operates. But my New York Latino brothers realized I was getting comfortable. So, they paid me a visit and said, "It's time for you to come back." That "coming back" paid off a few years later with the creation of Alianza Islamica, an organization in the Spanish Harlem neighborhood we grew up in.

The drug dealers on the block didn't like our presence, but we wanted to clean up that block, which led to confrontations. And one major one.

We were all held up in our little storefront, right at street level. We waited for an attack. We didn't know what was going to happen. We didn't know whether the drug dealers were going to bust the windows or spray the place with bullets. But we felt we had to be there to make a stand, come what may. If it was our time, then it was our time, but we made our stand. We prevailed that day and, alhamdulillah, we cleaned up that block.

Remember, these were all young people. This is what the youth had to deal with to establish Islam. Now we're past that time. That was 30 to 40 years ago. I don't know if your parents ever discussed those times with you, or if even if you had parents that were Muslim from that period. But it was a reality for most of us that we endured.

I will try to conclude. I've just taken you through a brief journey of my time, a very brief journey. During the time I lived with people who were also young and full of dreams and aspirations. The truth is that I'm old now. And my energy has waned, and my joints are reminding me that the car is stopping soon. I get trotted out from time to time to give a history lesson, which is probably the only thing I'm good at now.

But those who came before you were inspired in their time to actively seek change. They were not afraid to use the word revolutionary. And I don't mean in the sterile contemporary usage of a "revolution in razor blades." I mean a seismic paradigm shift in social, political, and economic relations that affect all spheres of life. Many early young Muslims who tried the promises of socialism, Black, and Latino militancy, and extreme national and racial pride have found all those systems wanting. Only Allah's deen, Islam, provides a total solution encompassing every facet of life, most importantly the spiritual, the one thing that seems to be missing from every other system, the one thing that actually makes better people, devoted servants of the Lord, Most High. You young people that are here, what will your story be in 40 years? Take notice of this and heed. You're writing it now.

Thank you. Assalamu Alaikum wa Rahmatullah.

Jose Acevedo:

I didn't say at the beginning. This is my father-in-law, my wife's father. We have a few minutes for questions and answers. Any comments? Please feel free. Take advantage of this opportunity. And he's going to be going back to New York, so we want to make sure that if you have any questions or comments, please ask now. Nothing? Yes.

Speaker 3:

What would you say is important for young people to know about to stay encouraged in their hearts and face adversity.

Rahim Ocasio:

First of all, anything that's going to happen is Allah's will. So, if you're in a tight situation, you don't know the outcome, but Allah knows the outcome. And whatever is going to happen is going to happen. So, you either survive that situation or you don't.

A Newyorican Odyssey

By Rahim Ocasio

My story began on a Sunday night in June 1953. At St. Francis Hospital in the South Bronx, I was born Ramón Francisco Ocasio to newly-arrived Puerto Rican parents. They had come for the grand American adventure, to the City of Nueva York, the land of milk and honey, where the streets were paved with gold. But they had to settle for the fifth floor of an old tenement on 110th Street and Madison Avenue in Manhattan's Spanish Harlem.

The fabled ghetto, known to the locals affectionately as El Barrio, was, at the time, the cultural and spiritual heart of the Puerto Rican community in New York as well as the country. Boricuas slowly but inexorably made their way from Fifth Avenue to the East River, displacing and often fighting its prior residents, the Italians, for every block. West Side Story was in those days as much a documentary as it was a musical.

My parents were Roman Catholic, as were most of those of the Boricua diaspora. But Espiritismo, a remnant of ancient African religions intermingled with Catholicism, was strong in my household. Our back room was a kind of altar replete with all the trappings of the African cult: velas (religious candles), busts of the black Siete Potencias, El Indio, and el Buddha pipón, dried out apples, corn, and palm leaves. This contrasted with the traditional religious training I was receiving from the Irish Christian Brothers at Commander Shea, St. Cecilia's annex on 111th Street. My Catholic school teachers denounced pagan African traditions, while orthodox Roman Catholic teaching was put forward as a bulwark against encroaching heathenism.

I was comfortable with this orthodoxy, however. Visiting priests heard confessions every Thursday in preparation for Friday and Sunday masses. Sunday mass was obligatory, attendance taken, and summary beatings administered Monday if excuses were not satisfactory. I found the annual street processions, novenas, Stations of the Cross, and deeply sentimental religious holiday celebrations warmly comforting. By the time I was in the sixth grade, I was contemplating the priesthood, eventually becoming an altar boy who would wake up on cold winter mornings to serve St. Cecilia's six o'clock mass to a surprisingly substantial crowd of devotees.

When I was about 12, I had a noteworthy experience. I was due to receive the sacrament of Confirmation on a Sunday, and for some reason, I was not in attendance the previous Thursday at the chapel to confess. We couldn't receive the sacrament unless we were free of sin, so I would have to make a Saturday trip to St. Cecilia's, the parish church, to have my confession heard.

But I arrived too late, the priests had all gone home, and now I was in a pickle. However, I reasoned that since God is all-knowing and ever-present, I would appeal to him directly to forgive my sins. I prayed to Him exclusively as it never occurred to me due to my Catholic religious training to direct any requests to Jesus or the Holy Ghost. The next day I was confirmed as a Christian soldier and received the ceremonial slap with no misgivings about my direct appeal to God. Years later, I would reflect on the significance of that day.

My high school years were filled with challenging religious debate as this was the '60s, and even our Religion teachers at my Catholic high school were questioning long-held ideas. I was also having spirited discussions with the half of my family that were Pentecostals, whom I viewed at the time to be anti-intellectual and close-minded. All this would change radically as I transitioned from high school to college.

In 1969, I met a young 14-year-old named Mark Ortiz, wearing a purple beret, and spouting a barrage of socio-politico-economic aphorisms, which left me dizzy. As far as I could tell, he was the youngest member of a new force in El Barrio that would forever change it: the Young Lords Party.

Originally a gang out of Chicago, it had adopted Marx-Leninist-Maoist political ideology and a community service tactic that resembled the Black Panther Party in many ways. And the bewildering aphorisms my new young friend had spouted were beginning to make sense. In 1970, by the time I was 17, the former altar boy and priesthood aspirant was selling Palantes, the party paper, advocating socialist revolution, an end to capitalist imperialism, freedom for Puerto Rico, and the abolishment of that great opiate of the masses: religion.

Everything pointed to the fact that radical action was necessary. My beloved El Barrio had turned into a hell-hole of drugs and violence. Typically, getting to the front door of my fifth-floor apartment meant stepping over several stoned, often vomit-covered junkies who used my floor as a shooting gallery. Blood smeared the walls, and the floor, which hadn't been swept or mopped in years, was littered with discarded "duji" or heroin bags. Long abandoned by the landlord and taken over by the City, my apartment building would see entire winters with no heat and hot water. Ceiling collapses injured my mother and brother, and so much violent death surrounded us that we became eerily detached from its horror.

So, a radical revolution seemed to be the solution along with its atheistic socio-political rhetoric. My college social science courses, SS10 and 11, which I would later call ATHEISM 101, reinforced this view. It viewed religion as just mankind's way of explaining the natural world, a progression from primitive animism and nature worship to monotheism with the implication that these simplistic explanations for natural phenomena were superseded by science. I was right at home on my soapbox in the neighborhood preaching atheism, helping tenants carry out rent strikes, taking the night watch at university building take-overs, marching by torch-light behind a hapless effigy, or demonstrating at the UN.

However, I started to feel something was not right. It was not with the revolution but the revolutionaries. With all the ideological training and good intentions, not enough attention was being paid to the development of character. Guys and girls cheating on each other, and frequent drug use made me wonder what to expect of this brave new world re-made.

Dissatisfied with the direction of the "movement," I continued my search. It wasn't clear to me yet, but I was searching for something. I was searching for answers before I even knew what the questions were. Now, with a friend's encouragement, I was exploring the beliefs of the Nation of Islam. Malcolm X had been dead for nearly seven years, but the movement he had helped build was still a force in Harlem and had captured the imagination of a great many people. Based on the belief that the black man was the original man, father of civilization, and god of the universe, it broadly encompassed virtually all non-whites. However, it conferred a special status on those with purer black bloodlines.

I never became a Black Muslim, but I wound up joining a group that took their beliefs to their logical conclusion. The Five Percenters, a breakaway group started by a dissident Black Muslim named Clarence 13X, believed that if God was the original man, the Black Man, then it followed that godhood was invested in all black men collectively. Submitting to one man as Muslims must be an absurdity. I became one who believed that there was nothing in the universe greater than oneself, embodying the ultimate in arrogance, the apex of delusion, the consummate atheist deluxe.

The news came to us that Mark Ortiz, the young 14-year-old who first opened my eyes to political struggle as a Young Lord had become a Muslim. My friend John and I were furious and went promptly to his house and spent what must have seemed like hours deriding him for becoming a Muslim and telling him how stupid he was for doing so.

We hurled abuse at him non-stop for being such a jerk, but he simply smiled, totally unfazed. Nothing we could say or do shook him in the slightest away from his faith in Allah. To us, he was the biggest "sangano" in El Barrio. But he met our fury with a calm serenity that only true faith could bring about. It was something we had never seen before, and it foreshadowed things to come.

One day, at a gathering at Pueblo, the Latino club at Fordham, Lincoln Center, I was engaged in a spirited discussion with one Federico Lora. Federico was one of the mainstays of a progressive group called El Comite. He was intelligent and well-regarded. In one of the seminal blunders of my entire life, I tried to explain to him a tenet of Black Muslim belief; how white people were created out of test tube by a black scientist named Yaqub on the island Patmos in the Aegean Sea.

He laughed in my face.

I had no retort. I realized how ridiculous I was sounding. I felt awkward, rudderless.

My belief in the most bizarre of cosmologies had brought me to the emptiest of feelings. And the rationalization that I was the pinnacle of creation, a god of the universe, brought no solace or comfort. What do you do for an encore once you have been deified?

I had hit rock bottom.

Not long after, I attended a Kwanzaa celebration. Amidst the gaiety of traditional food, dance, and song, I was oddly detached. I turned and looked up at a paper plate stuck to the wall with the words written in a semi-circle around it, "You are what you eat, physically, materially, and spiritually."

Spiritually. I remained fixated on that word. I hadn't contemplated anything remotely spiritual in years. I had been an avowed dialectical materialist now converted to the most atheistic religion on the planet. Cynicism and skepticism about anything remotely spiritual or esoteric were embedded in my personality. But it didn't feel quite right to be a dispassionate, unfeeling automaton. Cold logic seemed just that: cold.

The turning point came when I attended an event that featured a recently released Puerto Rican political prisoner. After the event, a man walked up who seemed familiar. I then remembered him from two previous occasions. His name was Abdullahi, a Boricua Muslim from the East River projects. Almost two years earlier, he tried to explain his religious philosophy so bizarrely that I thought he was advocating tree worship. The other occasion was quite different. He stepped up to the microphone at a Young Lords rally at the Hunts Point Palace in the Bronx and gave a stirring speech about the importance of a social conscience.

Now this enigmatic man began to speak to me about a fascinating new way of looking at the world, a novel belief, and a new way of life he called Islam. Not the custom-made distortion of Islam espoused by the Black Muslims but something new and intriguing. His words touched me in a way that is difficult to explain. His words were filling that gaping spiritual void in my heart, and I was drawn to his message.

But I was still cautious. I was intrigued by his invitation to explore Islam, but I was emphatic that I was not interested in anything "spooky." By that, I meant any fanciful, illogical religious hocus-pocus. In many ways, I was still the skeptical materialist, on guard against anything mystical or irrational. If I were going to accept any new belief, it would have to be based on logic and reason. I didn't want to be hoodwinked again.

Abdullahi suggested my search for Islam start at the main branch of the public library on 42nd Street, one of the world's largest reference libraries. My trips to the library were very interesting. These were the pre-computer days of card catalogs and the Dewey Decimal System. Books had to be looked up in the card catalog, and requests were written down and handed to the attendant who would procure your books. Abdullahi had apprised me that the truth of Islam was carefully hidden from the general population. The attendants at the reference section of the

Oriental department would not be too cooperative in obtaining our requests. Just as he predicted, we only received about half to two–thirds of our requests. I was intrigued and wanted to know more about what I perceived was deliberately kept from me.

I began to attend the mosque regularly, even started to take Arabic classes. I spent almost all my spare time with Abdullahi and his Cuban companion Khalil (Carlito). One Friday evening, I attended a lecture at Ya Sin mosque in Brooklyn with my lifelong friend Johnny who had been with me during my days running the streets, my Marxist politicization, and pseudo-deification. At the end of the lecture, we were invited to accept Islam. There was a not so subtle "threat" that there were no guarantees in life or that we would even make it to the subway station, so we should consider becoming Muslims to safeguard our hereafter. One of our companions who brought us urged us not to bow to any pressure to accept Islam and only to do it when we were good and ready.

Later on, that evening, it hit me in a grocery store of all places; there was no reason left for me not to become a Muslim. The comprehensiveness of the message had sealed it for me. My spiritual and religious questions were answered in the Unity of the Divine Being, Allah, and a coherent history of prophetic continuity, ending with the Prophet Muhammad. It was now clear where both Judaism and Christianity, in fact, all previous religions, went astray and why Islam was the culmination of revelation. Islam also allayed my fears that it would create a withdrawn, anesthetized society unresponsive to life's challenges and inequities. It was a comprehensive system that had answers for every field of life, be it social, political, economic, juridical, or familial. It aspired to create a rational society based on faith in the One God and devoted to justice and the common good. The altar boy and the revolutionary were now reconciled. It was time to evolve.

John and I resolved that the next day we would take the shahada and become Muslims. The rest of that night, I was restless. That whole night I practiced making the prayer and studying the little Arabic I had learned. The next day, March 10, 1973, at the 125th Street mosque, we affectionately called 303, the place reportedly where Malcolm X prayed his last Asr salat before meeting his fate at the Audubon, John and I took our shahadas and became Muslims.

My parents were very accepting of my conversion. Considering how things were in El Barrio at the time, they seemed relieved that I was not going to wind up a junkie or "un bandido". But one day, I can't remember how it started, my father and I got into heated words in my living room. I grabbed the bust of El Indio, a fixture for decades in our backroom Espiritista altar, and threatened to smash it against the floor. I asked my father if he really believed that a thunderbolt would come through the window and strike me down if I had done so. I turned it over and showed him the label. I told him that bust itself was a manufactured thing with absolutely no power. He simply told me that he didn't deride my religion and that I had no right to deride his. That ended the argument.

Sometime later, we were moving to a new apartment, and I showed him the idols that were now confined to a bureau drawer. "Pop, what do you want me to do with these?" I asked. He replied, "Dejalos.". And with that, no idols were ever seen in our house again.

In time, both my parents were to accept Islam, my father as he was dying of cancer, and my brother. My ex-girlfriend from college accepted Islam, and we were married less than two months before our Fordham University graduation. Three months later, her sister took shahada on the day I left for Washington, DC, to join the Islamic Party and continue a struggle I had started long ago. But now I was armed with a powerful ideology based on truth and the guidance of the Supreme Being.

Several years after my return from Washington, my old friend John, now known as Yahya, and I fulfilled a dream of starting a Latino Muslim organization. Alianza Islamica, in its heyday, was the premier Latino Muslim organization on the East Coast and quite possibly the country. Though today it is but a memory, it is still fondly remembered. Now there are many more Latino Muslims than there were in the early days, and they are more diverse. There were so few of us in those early days, and being Latino was virtually synonymous with being a Newyorican. My hope, inshallah, is that succeeding generations surpass us in every way and that Islam among Latinos grows and develops its own unique presence.

I have been blessed with eleven Muslim children, seven sons, four daughters, and grandchildren, a fine and blessed legacy, alhamdulillah. But I feel humbled when I reflect that it all began on a Sunday night in the South Bronx, nurtured on the fifth floor of a tenement at 1648 Madison Avenue on 110th Street, with an insignificant, undeserving, nearsighted, brown-skinned, buck-toothed Boricua.

All praise is due to Allah, Lord of all the Worlds.

At the Mosque of Islamic Brotherhood (MIB)

This panel about NYC Latino Muslims, specifically about Alianza Islamica, occurred at the Mosque of Islamic Brotherhood (MIB) in Harlem. The panel consisted of Yahya Figueroa, Rahim Ocasio, and Ibrahim Abdul Aziz.

Yahya Figueroa:

Assalamu Alaykum wa Rahmatullahi wa Barakatuhu. That's more like it.

Alianza Islamica was known for its lack of support because we had the audacity. We had the audacity to speak for ourselves without looking for any validation or approval from anyone. And that was audacity. Being a colonized people, being under the control of someone else's domination and understanding, the nature of a colonized mentality, we did not come to Islam to be spiritually colonized. Real simple, we entered into Islam already having a movement orientation. In other words, for us, the vacuum was a spiritual vacuum. There was a spiritual dilemma. And when that spiritual dilemma was filled upon hearing that hey, there is Allah, there is a power that you can tap into, and that power was Allah, which has left us without the spiritual malady.

We now have a political idea of where we were, where we came from, and what we need to do. And with the spirit of accepting Islam, we understood what we want for ourselves and what we want for our people. And this comes from the tradition of resistance, a tradition of struggle because nothing changes if nothing changes. Our brothers, our peers who trained us, our African American brothers, always felt an affinity between the Boricua and the African American. We come from the tradition of the

400 years of slavery and understand that tradition well and identify with their struggle. There are similarities and slight differences like language. Another might be culture. But in essence, we share a common history. That commonality, we always promoted. We coexisted. We were orphans within Islam. Islam had already had generations amongst African- Americans.

One of the first times I'd heard new words like Allah or anything Islamic, these new words were when I was 11 years old, and it was the Five-Percent Nation. That was my first introduction to Allah, the name Allah. It didn't mean very much to me then, but later, Allah would appear again. So, I'm not so critical as to the evolution of how Islam came about in this country. It's a history we may like or not. That's irrelevant. It is our history.

As a former member of the Young Lords myself, I mostly worked with high school students through the Third-World Student League, a subsidiary of the Young Lords. We did a lot of student organizing. We then were introduced to Marxism and this notion of being an atheist, and that's wherein the problem lies. We parroted these lines, but we were a spiritual people with spiritual traditions. So, there was always a vacuum. We took the Young Lords' template, and that of the Black Panthers, and combined it with Islam. Putting it together, we said, "Man, we got a program. We have an idea. We have a methodology of the da'wah." The da'wah was not just inviting people to Islam, per se. We didn't want that approach.

We wanted to develop a relationship with our community, which was imperative. We also wanted to develop relationships with other progressive organizations. We were never so self-righteous that we couldn't work with other people who were not Muslim. You see, so this notion of "wala wa bara," a concept of disassociation, everything is haram. Music is haram. Your clothing is haram, and being Puerto Rican is haram. I'm very passionate about this because you can see the level of ignorance. We struggled to maintain our identity.

In other words, I am a Muslim and a Puerto Rican unapologetically who happens to be a Muslim. I have multiple identities, and so what? To me, how important is Islam if it doesn't have any culture? All knowledge must be culturally based. The foundation of all knowledge must have a cultural foundation. We understood this. How is it possible that we would cower to another oppressed people suffering from the same political situation and expect them to guide us? How is that possible?

We struggled with Puerto Rican Muslims who had accepted Islam, who had a problem bringing it back home. They were immersed in other communities, whether it was Tablighi Jamaat or others. They just took on a different identity because they were told to change your culture. In a sense, I am a victim because of my ignorance, because someone told me I had to change my name. So, I gave up my name, John Anthony Figueroa, and legally changed it to Yahya Abdul Latif. Now I tell new Muslims, "Whoever told you have to change your name is mistaken. This is not a requirement of din. It's not a requirement." Of course, others say, "Well, he's wrong. You have to change your name." So anyway, these are some of the struggles that we went through.

Others question how it is possible that a Puerto Rican can lead an organization. How is that possible? Did he get credentialed from somewhere in the Middle East? Did someone give him approval? Does one have to validate him? When I went to Hajj, I had to be "certified" by someone in the Islamic Center to make Hajj. Again, we're reduced to second-class Muslims.

My contribution to Alianza Islamica was that of a radical: instigating, agitating, and promoting Alianza Islamica. When people would come to Alianza Islamica, we wanted to know not how much Islam they knew. When I came to Islam, it was simple. You learn ten little surahs. You learn how to pray and speak to your Lord. You learn about wudu. And you don't have to immerse yourself and waste 30 years in something that is not going to help you. There are those amongst us who exceed, and this is a calling for them. But not everyone has to pursue this course.

The pressure was put on people to do all this learning in study circles. A lot of these brothers died with nothing. They detached themselves from their families because they were told not to participate in family affairs. This behavior caused a lot of destruction.

Alianza Islamica looked at the community. We determined its needs. Well, we had a drug problem here. How are we going to address that drug problem? Well, we have to clean it up. It's our community, not a ghetto. It's where we live.

We began to address that, and of course, because we were not, say, orphans and strangers in El Barrio, we made alliances with people that were Young Lords in the past: the Puerto Rican Forum, the Puerto Rican Congress. We started making alliances and when we had a problem on Rikers Island, a lot of slashings, they wanted me to see what I could do.

I went to Lewisburg Penitentiary and met some of the inmates there. They were former gang members. I explained to them the dilemma, and they said, "Don't worry about it. This stops now." I was able to stop the riots there. People who were members of the Latin Kings wanted to become Muslim. I don't call them gangsters. I call them street organizations. Why? Because I was there. I was a gang banger, and I understand their language. So, I took it to them in a language they understood. And as a result, many of those people would come to me and ask, "Why would a Latin King become a Muslim?" My answer to them is because we answer to a higher authority. It's an upgrade.

We made this little kufi with the gold and black colors, and we said, "Here, we're going to give you this kufi. Wear it." This is wisdom. We're not beating them down, and we're not judging them. We meet them where they are. But for you to have this relationship, you must invest time in people. The dawah mentality of putting out tables and fliers is a waste of time, a waste of time. You have to engage the people. The people will tell you what you must do. You don't have to tell them what to do. Our people already know what the problem is. It is our job to be able to see their problem and be able to articulate it for them. And if we're going to use Islam, then we must look for solutions within Islam to remedy some of their problems. Lack of education, I got you. People came in with no high school diplomas. Some of them walked away with double masters. That to us is da'wah. Where's the transformative power of Islam? What is this recklessness of converting people to Islam, leaving them on the wayside to further destroy themselves? Reckless.

I've seen a lot of cyber organizations, a lot of talking heads. My question to them is straightforward. One, who is mentoring you? Who are you? Because you went and acquired a piece of paper wherever you received it, that qualifies you for some leadership position? It doesn't work that way. Our tradition is building movements from the ground up, not an elitist belief that a piece of paper entitles you to leadership.

I am who I am. I am not a scholar of Islam, but I had the good sense to get some qualified people. We never put these people upfront. So, everybody said, "Well, this is just Yahya. So, what the hell does he know about this deen? But in the background, we had Brother Ibrahim Abdul Aziz and Brother Sharif Abdul Karim. We have brothers who were already not only educated Islamically but had a little secular education. Because there are people who have a GED maybe and claim to be able to understand archaic Arabic, classical Arabic. How is that possible? They haven't even mastered English. And we fall for the hokey dope.

Fire is wrong when it's in the wrong place. Put in the right place, it is cooking a meal. In other words, scholarship is important if put in the right place. A lot of us get mesmerized, so we demystified the notion of a scholar as an all-knower. That's dangerous thinking. In Alianza Islamica, we took the professionals and put them where they needed to be. People wanted to learn Puerto Rican history; many didn't even know their history. I did the simplest thing. I went to Hunter College and found the director of the Puerto Rican history department. I said to him, "Listen, I'm recruiting you to give a class at Alianza Islamica, and you're not going to get paid."

And guess what? The response was, "Yahya, if you ask us to do this, I'm down." Why? Because it's called social credibility. You develop social credibility and have credit with people. Through what? Your contributions, your reputation.

PRACA is one of the largest Puerto Rican organizations in America, founded by Yolanda Sanchez. It is also a person who is also responsible for formulating Aspira, another Puerto Rican organization around for years. I stepped up to Yolanda Sanchez, and said, "Yolanda, I'm here at your service. I am a Muslim. How can we collaborate?" "Okay, fine. Would you do security for the Muevete Conference?" which was to be a massive event. We provided security. What's the next step? "Would you give a workshop on Islam?" In other words, we didn't come in demanding anything. It was demanded of us.

Ray Barreto, a famous Puerto Rican musician, once said, "Would you please educate my children about Islam?" You see, this is something earned. It was natural and organic. It wasn't a systemic or cookie-cutter version of Islam. It was adjustable, flexible, and malleable so that you could speak in the people's language.

King Tone was the leader of the Latin Kings and got caught up on the RICO act. I believed he was on the verge of making a radical change. But we continue to network with them. When we had problems in the street, or with the properties we were managing, he was there to assist.

We managed a PRACA building where we were providing tutoring for the children. We had a member named Muhammad Mendez. May Allah elevate him to the highest. Wow, what a tremendous soldier. He and his wife took on the duty of tutoring women who had lost their children to the system and reentered them into this dwelling that we were asked to manage.

We managed that. We set up these teachers, who aided them with their homework, helping them to excel. Once a member of the Latin Kings trespassed into that building and refused to leave. And I said, "Look, I'm just telling you, no men are allowed in the building. You should leave the building." So again, making connections, I called King Tone. I said, "King Tone, I got a dilemma here. I got a guy in one of my buildings that doesn't want to move out."

He said, "I'll be there in 10 minutes." I didn't call the police. This is just community collaboration, community cooperation. We're helping each other. And so, I'm calling them to do something good for Muslims. Let's look at them as Ansars, as helpers. We believe in that, helpers. Listen, God blessed us that we have freedom of choice. You don't have to be a Muslim. Let that be a conscious decision, something that you want to do. Don't let anyone coerce you into Islam. We have to provide convincing arguments not because Islam says so but a persuasive argument. Why should I be a Muslim? What has it done for you? So anyway, King Tone comes over. This woman is pregnant, and her boyfriend is dead.

And so, King Tone tells them, "Listen, when this baby is born, you're going to be six feet under, as soon as the child is born."

And I said, "Wait a minute, no, whoa, whoa, whoa, whoa. We want justice. We believe in justice. That's a little exaggerated. All I want this man is to leave the building. We don't need all of that." But this is developing a relationship with someone who has a huge following. They have these parliaments where they get together, and I'm looking at all these 17 and 16-year-olds, and I'm looking at how I can get these people empowered? How could I try to provide some direction, some structure? I don't have a whole lot of time to debate with Muslims whether we should go left or right. It's a waste of time, arguing issues of aqidah. Listen, we have more important things to think about. We're human. We're a work in progress. The idea that I have this perfect outlook on what Islam is and what it's not. Listen, all I know is that I'm alive only because of Allah. I have five minutes the sister says, and I'm very respectful of time.

We set up HIV programs, substance abuse programs, a GED program, and a gang intervention program. We had an oppressed people's affairs committee. Some people handled political issues. The decolonization of Puerto Rico was a major issue. We also visited the prisons. We also set up a recovery meeting for recovering addicts because that was plaguing our community. We held parental guidance classes. We initiated sewing classes for sisters. I mean, you name it, and we did it. We sold verduras. We sold shoes. We did whatever we had to do to sustain ourselves.

I'll leave with this. Every time I get on this microphone, I think about all the brothers and sisters who are no longer with us. It is mind-boggling to me, the work that these people put forward. It's unbelievable. I am just a little dust mote in Alianza Islamica. I was privileged to be part of that movement. It was a little atom, but very powerful. We were there for each other. When brothers came into Islam, we didn't sit around in circles learning Islam. Listen, this brother died. Let me teach you how to wash his body. OJT, without the luxury about this bourgeoisie mentality that we're going to learn Islam academically, no. This is OJT. We mentored people. We made sure that people called in every day for a status check to ensure they were okay. We looked out for each other. We worked as a unit. For 14 years, we did this. People are talking about replicating it, but it hasn't happened yet, because they want to reinvent the wheel when there's plenty of work to do. All they have to do is be willing to do the work and stop theorizing.

We don't need a methodology. We already have something functional, viable, proven to work. If people were to establish little communities in all the major cities, you would see a positive transformation. You would see the impact and influence of Islam in the Latino community. That's all I have.

Thank you.

Rahim Ocasio:

Assalamu Alaykum wa Rahmatullah wa Barkatuhu. Hard to follow that up. That was quite an introduction. I've known him since he was 13 years old. We used to live across the street from each other on 110th Street and Madison Avenue. It's a long history. We were in the streets doing what people do in the streets. And then we got caught up in the movement. I'd like to provide some kind of historical context here.

The '60s and '70s were explosive times. Those who lived during them remember that. I lived in probably the worst building that you could imagine. I had to walk over junkies to get over to my front door, blood-smeared walls everywhere. Yahya here remembers. It was a horror show with ceiling collapses, and no garbage pickup. I went for years with no heat and hot water. I kept my baby bassinet just to fill it with hot water so that I could take a bath. That's how bad it was.

So naturally, a powder keg that was ready to explode, and it did. And though we were teenagers, when the movement came calling, it fired our imagination. We went with it full speed. Yahya, Ibrahim, and I were no more than 17 years old. Eventually, we took part in university building takeovers and were the first watches at Columbia, and City

University's City College. We got caught up in a Marxist, Leninist, Maoist philosophy. It was atheist, and we began to see that there was a spiritual vacuum. We knew we were looking for something. Yahya and I became Five-Percenters, and we had everything memorized, the Actual Facts, the Mathematics, everything they had. I memorized everything.

One day, I went to a Kwanza during that time, and I looked up at a paper plate on the wall that had written on it, "You are what you eat spiritually, mentally, and physically." Spiritually? I hadn't thought about spirituality in a long time. And that really hit me. Not long after that, we met a brother that brought us to Islam. I had met that guy before, but he was so cryptic in the way he explained Islam, I thought he was talking about worshiping trees. But this time, he was lucid. He made more sense, and after that, we shortly became Muslim. On the same day. Yahya and I are joined in that way, March 10, 1973, at the same masjid that reportedly Malcolm made his Asr before he went up to the Audubon, which doesn't exist anymore, 303 125th Street.

From there, we joined the Islamic Party together, a revolutionary organization at that time, and the first place where we learned what it was to be in a disciplined Islamic movement. Alianza Islamica didn't come out of a vacuum. It was a progression. It was a progression of an attitude of Islamic-driven movement, an Islamic-driven movement trying to move forward, trying to make a difference in the community, trying to change the community, trying to provide services for the community in an organized, structured, and disciplined way.

After our sojourn with the Islamic Party, then came Alianza Islamica. Alianza Islamica was unique because when Yahya and I talked about having a center in El Barrio, we didn't want to replicate what had already existed. Many imams took their positions almost as if they were the khalifa of Spain. It was more like storefront kingdoms and ghetto monarchies, and we wanted no part of that. Yahya and I talked about that, and we agreed that we were not going to have anything like that. We were going to have a different approach. We wanted a center in El Barrio, maybe a storefront, unassuming, that we could just bring people in, no royal trappings of kingship or monarchy or anything like that. We wanted to keep it simple. We want to keep it informal. We just want to bring people in to talk to them as an organic part of the community, and we've made that decision right from the very beginning.

We were fortunate to do it in Manhattan, away from the chaos of Brooklyn. We didn't want to be tied into the politics there. Our one ally was from this masjid, Imam Talib. He was the one ally, and we're glad that we had him and didn't have to deal with anybody else. We were able to grow on our own independently. We wanted to make a Latino expression just like Afro-Americans had done before us. But it was a barrier for Latinos because they felt they had to change their whole culture. They had to change the way they talked, acted, and dressed. We're Westerners. I'm a Westerner. I am not from the east, and I am not going to pretend that I am.

And people say, "Well, this is sunnah."

I responded, "The Prophet (peace be upon him) never dressed like that." Read your history." This is an approximation at best, but it's not what he wore. He dressed like the people from his area. We wanted to make an expression of Islam that didn't make people go through hoops simply to become Muslim. It had to be something that they could relate to, something that my mother could relate to. My mother accepted Islam, and my father before he died, Alhamdulillah. And so did Yahya's also, Alhamdulillah. But that may not have happened if you had to be somebody else. We're not going to be somebody else. We are who we are. We just accept Islam, and that's it.

That's why when we had our Eids, they reflected who we were. We brought congas in there. We ate our own dishes. By that time, we were sick of curry, so we had to have something a little different, some arroz con gandules or some pasteles, or something. I mean, it's just a reality. We had to have our expression of what the deen was, or it wouldn't make sense to people. They would not relate to it. That was very important. And to be able to do that, you must be a little bit of a rebel. Yahya and I were rebels. You must stand up for the people. You have to be yourself. You have to stand up for people who will not stand up for themselves.

Otherwise, who would speak up for them? Who would? Nobody. I would go to give dawah to Latinos on Columbia Road in Washington, DC as a member of the Islamic Party and was told, "You're on your own, buddy." And we realized, yeah, we are on our own.

So, if we wanted to go out into the community with a face that's familiar enough to get people to say, "Okay, I can relate to this, and maybe I can consider becoming Muslim," then there's no other choice. We'd have to do it, and we'd have to do it our way. We couldn't imitate any other model, because frankly, we didn't like the other models. We thought they sucked and thought we needed a completely different type of model if we were going to approach Latinos. Alhamdulillah.

How much time do I have?

It's important in the present day that we reevaluate how masjids are organized, how we view our leadership, how we view those people who we rely on for knowledge, and what knowledge they do claim to have.

I see a lot of communities in stagnation. They are not moving anywhere, and you must ask yourself, why? Why is that? Why are we kind of stuck in a quagmire? Why are we treading water? Why are we losing our youth? That's a big question. We have failed that next generation. We have to find a whole different way of engaging people. And actually, what is Islam? If Islam is not engaging the young, we've missed something. I mean, there's a fervor that converts have when they come to the deen. If that's not transferred to the kids, we've failed. Miserably.

Alianza Islamica was not perfect, but it did present a different approach that should be examined. It could provide an example of what could be. Yahya said it, engagement with people. How did I become Muslim, with a flier? I became a Muslim because somebody approached, talked, and appealed to me. That was Alianza's approach, a very personal approach. It was a conscious decision that we made because we felt that the previous models were not going to be adequate for us nor made any sense.

It had to be something different, and rebels do that. They break the mold. They want to do something different, do something out of the box. That's what Alianza Islamica was, something different and out of the box that was not going to follow any cookie-cutter model that we thought was wholly inadequate and inappropriate to our situation. Alhamdulillah, that's all I have to say.

Ibrahim Abdul Aziz:

I'm just going to quickly read what I did in my last khutbah, the brothers at Masjidul Kauthar in Newark, New Jersey, a small community, a very loving group of people. Since I've retired, I've realized that I had almost no relationship with the Holy Qu'ran. I think most of us need to work on that. So, try to read Qur'an every two weeks. Try to complete it every two weeks. The Prophet (peace be upon him) said in his last speech on Earth to his largest audience, "I've left with you two things. If you hold onto them, you'll never go astray: the book of Allah and the Sunnah of his Holy Prophet." So, we're going to review all the books of Sunnah, nine major books. Let's review those, many in English, many not.

I read last week for them a wonderful set of hadiths from a man named Darimi. Most books begin with Bukhari, Muslim, typically with the book of Iman, or the book of how the revelation began. Darimi begins in a very strange way. He begins with what was it like in the jahiliyyah before Islam came. What did Allah Almighty do to us by this religion he gave us, and what is the power bigger than any culture, bigger than any race, bigger than any language? What did Allah almighty give us that shines as bright as the sun in the sky? And that's what we judge all this stuff against. A man asked the Holy Prophet (peace be upon him) in the first hadith of Sunan al-Darimi, "Will a man or woman be judged by what they did before Islam in jahiliyyah?"

The Holy Prophet, (peace be upon him), responded, "Whoever is good in Islam will not be taken to account by what they did in the jahiliyyah. But whoever does evil in Islam will be taken to account for what they did in the jahiliyyah." Now we all know the normal hadith says everything is wiped out. But here you see Imam Darami saying, "Yeah, that's true, but be careful. Be careful."

Then Imam al-Darimi says in the next hadith that a man described how he behaved in the jahiliyyah. All of us have our own jahiliyyah, our own period of ignorance before Islam. Even as Muslims, there are periods when you don't have a relationship with the Holy Qur'an. When the angels come into the grave and say, "What did you say about this man of Muhammad?" and you say, "I said what everybody else said." That's not a good enough answer. That's not a good enough answer.

Anyway, he described how they were in the jahiliyyah. "Prophet of Allah, in our time of ignorance, we worshiped idols, and we used to kill our children. One day I took my baby daughter to a well that was close to where we lived. And I flung her into that well and killed her. I held her little hand, and her last words to me were, 'Baba, Baba, Father, Father, why?' But it didn't stop me from flinging her to her death. At this, the Holy Prophet wept profusely. A man, a Sahabah, with us said, 'Stop. Stop, you're distressing the Prophet of Allah.' To which the Prophet of Allah said to him, 'Leave him.' And he said, 'Repeat that story for me.' And the tears continued to soak down his beard onto his clothes as he listened to that cruelty. The Prophet of Allah then said to that man, 'Allah has overlooked the evil actions done in Jahiliyyah. But be very careful that you do good now.'"

Another tale describes the Jahiliyyah. A man said, "My people sent me with goods, among them butter and milk to deliver to the idols of their gods. But I was afraid to eat from the butter because it belonged to their gods. And I put the milk and the butter down. Now a dog came along, and he ate the butter, and he drank the milk. And then the dog urinated on the idols." He said, "And these were Isaf and Na'ila, the two most famous idols of Mecca that we were carrying." Or again in jahiliyyah, when a man traveled, he would take four stones with him. Three he kept, one to worship, one to chase dogs away and one was to kill his child if he needed to on the trip. "In Jahiliyyah, if we found a beautiful stone, we would worship it, and we would take it to a camel and place it between its legs. If the camel would urinate on it or put milk on it, then we would say that stone was extra special. and worship it even more." That's how ignorant they were in the Jahiliyyah.

In Bukhari, people were warned of the great haraj to come. The Arabs, didn't know what that meant and asked, "What does haraj mean?" If my memory is correct, haraj is an Abyssinian word. The Holy Prophet replied, "The haraj is murder such that the murderer and the murdered don't know why they're killing." In another beautiful hadith, he says, "When you see the amount of Amana, trustworthiness, gone, when your word is meaningless, then expect the final hour to come upon you."

I'm a popular preacher. That's what I do. I preach. One of the things I speak with Brother Yahya and others and preach about is asking yourself how many Muslims are your close friends? I can count them on one hand, Yahya mentions Sharif Abdul Karim who used to be part of this community. We were lifelong friends. When he died, I was his closest friend. But I always chastise myself now. Why was I not a better friend to you? Why was I not a better friend? Why was I not a better friend? So, I would also ask those questions, and remember the word for sahabah is friendship, companionship.

The Prophet of Allah began his relationship with his closest companion, Abu Bakr as Siddiq . His daughter said,

"There was not a day before Islam or after Islam that my father did not meet with the Holy Prophet and give salams between them." Deep and loving friendship, this I don't find. Neither is this level of relationship found in the household between our wives and children.

I'm not Salafi. I love these kids. If they say, "I'm following hadiths," well, we want to follow hadiths more than you. We want to follow hadiths inner and outer, what it means spiritually and what it means outwardly. It is so clear from hadiths that if you don't have friendship, bravery, compassion, and love for your people, you have nothing from the Sunnah. What Sunnah would you be talking about? We should love Sunnah, and put into practice every hadith, every Sunnah, we find. Let's love it more than those kids love it.

I'll make this the last thing, stop my preaching. The great Shaykh Abdul Qadir Jilani, one of our great spiritual masters, said, "When you have an Islam with no spiritual inside, you're like the guy in the grocery store. He shows up at the counter. He got a big basket. He got an empty egg container, empty milk container, empty juice container. His whole shopping cart is empty. There's nothing there, and so it is with Islam if you have Sharia but no inner, no haqiqa, no tariqa, no nothing. You have an empty cart. You get up there with your empty stuff."

And so, I'd ask all of us, and I'm preaching to myself more than you, let's try to reestablish our connection to the Holy Qur'an. We all try to finish once at Ramadan. How often should you read Qur'an? The greatest Qur'an reader of all was a man named Ubayy ibn Kaab. The Holy Prophet (peace be upon him) said, "If you want to see Qur'an, take it from Ubayy. He is the one to read." Our master Ubayy used to finish in eight days regularly. But he said, "There were better than me. Tamim Dari, used to finish in seven days." It is said our khalifa Uthman ibn Affan, according to a Tirmidhi hadith, used to finish in one rak' ah of salah the entire Qur'an. It was a miracle. I don't think he did it every day, but it was a miracle. And it just shows what's possible if we push ourselves. Yahya and I have lived our whole lives in Islam. Our lives are like a cellphone on red. We're on red now. How much longer do we have to go? How much longer? I'll make it all connect. I'm like that when I try to talk. I don't say anything unless it's going to be from the Holy Koran or in the books of hadiths. I don't want to hear what no man has to say nor their opinions. I don't care about that stuff.

I had one of these young guys said to me, "Is that hadith a sahih hadith, is that a strong hadith?" I said, "For a dumbbell like me, anything in those great, old hadith books that our masters of hadith said is sahih enough for me. And I'm not a mufti. Any word that I find in Darimi or here, that's good enough for me. So, this young man said, "Is this sahih?". So let me ask you something. Well, when you go to the dentist or the doctor or wherever you go, do you ask him, "Is that 100%? Is everything you're doing 100%?" Or do you rely on the most likely or good enough to save your health and save your teeth.? We do that in our practical life, so we should do it in our faith. So, if I had anything to ask and plead for all of us, it's that we remake our connection to the Holy Qur'an, make our connection to the hadiths of the Blessed Prophet (peace be upon him), that we be humble pie as true and truthful Muslims for the rest our lives. We lived our whole lives. Let's live our lives. Let's pray that Allah Almighty will take our life and die in Islam, and be resurrected in Islam close to our Prophet, alayhis salam, that we drink from the Kauthar altogether in Jannah, and make of us people of the Holy Qur'an, people of the hadiths of our Prophet. (peace and blessings be upon him),

May He make us people that love and obey and be great neighbors and citizens, and people that inspired people to come to Islam by our example, by our words, by our lives and that he never let us be someone who chase people away from Islam by our bad behavior, bad judgment, lack of wisdom, lack of insight, or our egos.

Out of Bukhara comes one of the strongest and most beautiful hadiths in Bukhari Shareef. Imam Bukhari records that the Prophet of Islam (peace and blessing be upon him) said, "Lying about me is not like lying about anybody." But I think it also means when you start talking about religion and speaking any old nonsense, and you're claiming that that's coming from the Prophet of Allah and Islam, that's a form of lying on the Prophet of Allah. So, we should be careful. We should learn, again, the Prophet of Islam's (peace and blessings be upon him) hadiths. He says, "It's enough evil for a person that they say everything that comes to their mind."

We're all weak, and we all make terrible mistakes. And I'm worse than all of you, and I beg Allah Almighty that he bless your beautiful little masjid and that he blesses us all. We need a special Masjid al Kauthar. We need to reach out to all our second and third generation kids. Many of them are confused and have left Islam. I pray that Allah Almighty will help us find a way to keep them, bring them back, in whatever state of Islam they're in. The Prophet of Islam says, "Whoever says 'La ilaha illallah will enter into Jannah." When he was pressed on it by Abu Dhar Ghiffari, he said, 'If he does zina, and commits adultery and steals ...'' and on the third time, the Prophet said, 'Yes, he'll be in Jannah, if he says 'la ilaha illallah'. Even if you don't like it, he will be in Jannah.'" So, our mission is to get these kids to the masjid. If they can do that much, he can build on that if he can. That's all my preaching for you today. Thank you.

Rahim Ocasio:

I'd like to make one more comment. He was our spiritual anchor.

Ibrahim Abdul Aziz:

Please, don't bury me alive.

Rahim Ocasio:

I bring that up because they circulate stories about Alianza Islamica, that we were bringing people into Islam through music, like a Pied Piper to a conga beat. They tried to discredit and ...

Audience Member:

De-legitimize.

Rahim Ocasio:

Excuse me, sorry, de-legitimize us by saying that that's how we were approaching Islam. We were just bringing them in with music. I want to show, for the record, that we had strong spiritual anchors that were guiding Alianza Islamica all along.

Sister Yasmine:

We're going to segue into the question-and-answer session, and to do that, I'm going to first begin with answering one of the questions that you asked of us, which is, where are the children of the community? And oftentimes, if you want to test the community's health, the vitality of the community, you look to the children that they produced. And I can tell you that the children of Alianza, we are still in contact. We're still talking and playing, but most importantly, we are praying. And some of the programs that they did, feeding the community, the poor, the hungry, we see this continue. And to see so many of the children grown up now, continuing this, feeding bodies and spirits, this is the answer to your question. Estamos aqui. We're here.

Salwa Adly:

I appreciate the panel and thank you all for sharing your stories and your spiritual insight and wisdom. I can't help but notice the lack of a female voice here. And you want to talk about radical change at the grassroots level. Clearly, half of your population had to be female. What was that like in Alianza Islamica? What were, if you could tell us, some of the women's roles? Or maybe if you could even have one of the women share what their experience was. Because as profound, as impactful this statement was, I would love to have someone I could have identified with share their story about Alianza and how it impacted them as well.

Yahya Figueroa:

Well, I'll take a crack at it. Alianza Islamica looked at traditional values in terms of family. No, we were not feminists. Let's get this straight. Our sisters understood their place and their role, but Sister Maryam was the administrator, and brothers had to hear and take orders from her. Our sisters were public speakers, but they knew their place. They backed us up, and we backed them up, and we protected them. So, this whole idea of feminism, this feminism stuff is destroying our communities, destroying our families. This is not our agenda.

For all those who've been socialized in these institutions and been taught that we have a problem with men oppressing them, it is not an issue. It might be a Caucasian issue. It might be a white woman's issue, but it's not an issue that impacts us. Our job is to try to perpetuate the ideals of what makes a family functional. You can't have two people on the top regulating, creating confusion. In this constant battle, right now we have young sisters coming from these institutions who've been Muslim 15 years and would not marry. They say, "You know what? I'll just stay by myself. I'll just become a da'iah and propagate Islam all over the world. 'I'll become a spokesperson for Islam." But they will not marry. They will not have children. They will not take the responsibility of being a wife. This is a sure formula for the destruction of our families.

Ibrahim Abdul Aziz:

Well, I would just say that these are profound sociological ideas. We are in the middle of propaganda that goes on daily from the news, from here, from there. Our Islamic identity is a different thing entirely, and we need to preserve and protect it. One of the characteristics of our Holy Prophet was promoting a loving, caring family. And that means that everybody has their roles to play. And some time ladies might have a big role. Sometimes they don't. But I think we should be so careful. I would urge all of you. This is a vicious kind of propaganda war that is pitting our women and men against each other, just as blacks and Hispanics or blacks and whites currently are. All this propaganda is meant to rip us apart. That's why I say go back to the book of Allah Almighty. Go back to the hadiths of the Holy Prophet. You're a smart young lady. Read for yourself and see.

The story of the marriage of Khadijah to the Prophet of Islam is the foundational example of the Islamic family. Darami tells the story beautifully. When he came to her, his uncle, Abu Talib, said to him, "Look, go marry this girl. Work for her. Maybe marry her because we're uptight about money. We ain't got no money." And it was by her will, by her reputation, that Islam got its foundation. It gave him from the beginning moral support. So, was she in the back? Was she in the front? It was clearly a Muslim situation. So why don't we judge by this example?

I'll be honest with you. I'm always shocked that people are listening to these liars in the news. I ask, "How much time do you give to the Qur'an or hadiths of the Holy Prophet?" "I ain't got time for that." That's where the wisdom for us would be, not in these other things. Just because it sounds good when people talk like that, but everything comes out as good if you listen, but you don't see. Is this thing destructive to our Muslim communities, our Muslim households, and our Muslim children? It's something that needs great, great thought from us. We're representing the words of Allah Almighty in the Holy Qur'an.

Rahim Ocasio:

In our generation, we still had stable Latino families. Anything different would've created all kinds of disruption. The Islamic model and the Latino model have a lot of similarities. Actually, it came from there, because of our Andalusian history. So, there were fewer problems then. The generation after us has had a ton of issues because of the stuff he's talking about. Men and women, for some reason, don't know how to act with each other. The whole thing is breaking down, and it's not getting any better. That's why the phenomenon that Yahya was talking about is causing a lot of problems because now people cannot imagine that traditional Islamic model as a working model. And that is what has to be. Otherwise, we're finished.

Sister Yasmine:

I want to honor her question about where's the female voice? The female voice is where it's always been, right here. We're at their side. I was there. I was a little girl, but I was there. And before, I checked with one of the women that were there at the beginning and asked if she wanted to add, and she said she would be fine with me answering it. And I just want to check with the rest of the sisters that were there at the beginning - Is it okay for me to answer this question briefly?

Okay, so we weren't feminists there. We weren't chauvinists there. Alianza Islamica, my experience was that we were family-ists there. And that meant for the women's area, which was shared, was that it was a really rich and colorful experience filled with respect and energy. It was like una mezcla de Coran y khimars y coco helado y congas. It was all. It was a mix of it all. And that was what it was for me, and that was sort of the soundtrack and the rhythm that it was then. And it still carries on. Does that answer your question?

Salwa Adly:

Thank you.

Sister Yasmine:

Okay, you're more than welcome. Alhamdulillah. It was a great question.

Mikail asks, "How can our generation and the generation behind us build on the foundations that you established and support the work that you've done so that we can make you proud and make Allah happy?"

Yahya Figueroa:

Well, it's interesting, because, in Alianza Islamica, we did focus on the youth. For instance, we would take a lot of young people to the Poconos on weekends. So, we invested time in them. We also encouraged the brothers who were doing hip hop to continue doing the hip hop, to be able to express themselves when other communities say, "Listen, this hip hop thing is haram." But this is a way that the children were coming. And we're trying to take away the very thing that allows them to survive. And we tried to superimpose our ways on them without trying to understand, what is it that they want to do? Have we provided a safe space for the youth, spaces where they can facilitate their own programs, where we don't have to be dictatorial? Allow them to be organic. They're more than capable of providing an agenda for themselves. What we don't have is mentorship. There's a disconnect between the youth and their elders. That's something that's gone, but we need to establish mentorship. When I came to Islam, I had mentors. We just didn't become on our own. We had mentorship, for instance, the Dar al-Islam movement and MIB. These people were willing to mentor, teach, and help you. The youth have to bring in their agenda. We can discuss many things, including workshops.

For instance, what does it mean to have a girlfriend in the 21st century? How do we address those issues? Because the reality is that it is going to happen. We can't pretend it doesn't exist. We must address the issue of substance abuse amongst the youth. We know they use many medications. Many of our youth are overdosing. This is a concern.

What's driving them to substance abuse and self-destructive behaviors? Could we be supportive of one another? Where's the help for people who are struggling with those issues? Are we saying that they can't come to the centers and that we can't help them? We had referral services. For instance, we have the ability to, if you don't have the resources, refer them to someone else that can help. I think many of us now work with Millati Islami, a substance abuse program. And a lot of people were closed to that idea, but these are just some of the ideas I have. I don't have all the answers, but it begins by creating a safe space for yourself and having those discussions amongst yourself.

Ibrahim Abdul Aziz:

And so, for young people like yourself, my suggestion would be to try to find out where and in which of the masjids they have very professional Qur'an readers that you can go and sit with them, train yourself, and say, "I'm going to dedicate myself to learning to read the Holy Qur'an correctly." It's a wonderful project. Make that one of your things. When I was young, I went to Mecca and Medina. Get the young guys who are in groups and take off and go, because there're no words. There's nothing we can say up here to touch your heart and your Islam like seeing the Holy Kaaba and going to the Prophet's place. Nothing does that. So maybe organize those.

Another thing for you young guys; work out all this family relationship stuff, marriage, finding appropriate, little wives, and trying to get families to work. Because in my opinion, it's the number-one problem among all of our young people, the breakdown. And as Brother Yahya was just saying now, I'm amazed. God bless the da'wah sisters, anybody not married for 20 years. How can that be? You're going to into Islam. It's structured on the family. So, try to find out, I think, how we can make these families strong and protect our children. And again, all of us have had long histories and divorces, all of that stuff. Let's order the imams of these masjids. Order them. Say, "Hey, what are you going to do to help us work this problem out?" We need to do it. We need to have those sessions where we meet and try to figure out what the problem is. Are you married now if I could ask?

Speaker 8:

No, not yet.

Speaker 4:

Are you looking?

Speaker 8:

Mm-hmm (affirmative). .

Ibrahim Abdul Aziz:

So, these are good things to do, that you've been working on, and like what Yahya said, working on a strong financial foundation for yourself so that our people are prosperous. Young guys like you, I used to give khutbah to young people. If we don't make money to support our communities, who in the world is going to do it? It should be that you get out there and make our community as prosperous and wealthy as you humanly can. Young men are filled with ideas of power and youthful energy.t. Let's get out there and do it. That's what we need to do because, without that financial background, it'll be very tough. Allah Akbar.

Speaker 9:

Brother Rahim, you had mentioned about the transition that you brothers have made in your lives in terms of going from gang members to Five-Percenter, and then Islam. Now I know personally that most Latinos come from strong Catholic backgrounds. And most of the parents are stubborn when it comes to that. Because you also mentioned that your parents became Muslim, Alhamdulillah, and may Allah grant them Jannah. How did you brothers make that transition from the Five-Percent Nation, which was extreme, through those three phases? And how did your parents accept it though Islam was not as prevalent back then?

Sister Yasmine:

Okay, so for the viewers who are tuning in remotely, the question is directed towards Ramon Rahim Ocasio, how did you transition from your background of Catholicism into Islam? And how did that impact your family and your relations?

Rahim Ocasio:

Well, I did have a strong Catholic background. I went to a Catholic grammar school, high school, and college. I was an altar boy and used to serve mass at Saint Cecilia's on 106th Street, the 6 o'clock mass. And there was a good number of people there, as it was a more religious time. Before I became Muslim, through all my journeys, I was given a lot of latitude to search. When I became Muslim, my parents were happy, because I probably wasn't going to wind up a drug addict or dead. I lived at a time where every other guy was a junkie. It was a pandemic. There was a lot of death around me. A lot of people were dying. And for me to come and say that I'd become Muslim was greeted with relief. So even though I came from a strong Catholic background, the reality at the time was that this was good news compared to what the alternatives could've been. Alhamdulillah.

My father accepted my decision, even though he was still involved in a lot of Espiritismo, a Puerto Rican version of Santeria. We had some confrontations, but Alhamdulillah, he accepted Islam on his deathbed. And my mother had accepted Islam but wasn't practicing it. When my father died, she says to me, "Papo, what do we do now? What do I do now?" As this acknowledged that I am was now the male head of the household, I told her, "Now you practice Islam. You make your Salat. You do everything as you're supposed to do." And that she did. I was the eldest son and accepted my responsibility. She was turning over to me the mantle of authority. And I just told her, "This is how you're going to practice Islam from now on. You're going to be making all your Salats, and you're going to be conscious of your deen. And basically, that was the end of that story."

Yahya Figueroa:

We come into the world with fitra, our natural state. It's about reminding ourselves about that fitra. And yes, culturally, "Ahlan wa sahlan. Mi casa es tu casa'" a saying we have like ojala, inshallah. It is in the culture and can easily be detected. We can see the comparability between Islam and the culture within the Latino community. But mind you, we're a colonized, broken people. We have that thing called double consciousness. We suffer from that, so it's challenging. A lot of Puerto Ricans don't even know their history. That's sad. In Alianza Islamica, we called in the professor to show our history of resistance, that we resisted colonization and slavery in Puerto Rico. The slaves that we brought into this country were small in number. Most of them went to the Caribbean, Brazil, and Haiti. The number came to, perhaps, 500,000. But most of the slaves were spread throughout the Caribbean, so we have that history. We know that some slaves were also Muslims. They were educated Muslims and scholars of Islam. We need a non-euro-centric version of our history.

And a lot of people are writing about this history, so I think that in time Latinos will be able to see the similarities between Islam and their own culture. So, the family values, el padrino, la madrina, that's just an extended version of family. I will cut off with this. The biggest commodity in the Latino family is relationships, not money, nothing else, but relationships. In my house, there was always a stranger sleeping on the sofa. We were involved in helping one another. This is part of Islam. We are people of charity, and so you see that.

Donde como uno, comen dos. We are one people. One person eats, two people eat. Mama always put extra food on the table in case the visitor dropped in. We all expected it. It wasn't a selfish, hyper-individualistic type of lifestyle.

Sister Yasmine:

So, the question was, were you aware of what was happening at local masjids but particularly at MIB and the work we were doing here? And if you were, did it inspire you or help influence Alianza's movements in any way?

Yahya Figueroa:

Without a doubt. I came to MIB when Imam Talib was a teenager and Imam Taufiq right alongside him. So, I go way back. Alianza Islamica drew from the spirit of that tradition. Imam Talib has always been a mentor to me. Imam Talib was my go-to guy when we got into situations in the neighborhood. We consulted him. When I first took this job on, I went to Imam Talib and said, "Listen, I'm a layman. I would take this position if you could guarantee me that you got my back." See, I know how to rumble. I know I'm smart enough to have the right team in the right place. So, this allowed me to be bold. Do you want an Islamic debate? Well, do you know what? We got that for you. Let me go back here and get it. Here's the Islamic debate. Do you want to talk about HIV? Well, guys, here's our expert, Dr. Suni Ahmad. We always had experts. We knew quite well how to defer to scholarship, and everybody stood in their lane. And so yes, proactive in the community, Black Lives Matter, I mean we've always been. In fact, Palestine, political prisoners, whatever the challenges were, we took them on, because Muslims have a civic duty. Not just to preach theology.

What is your civic duty? What are you going to contribute to society? Theology? That's it? No, we weren't going to do that. We had to get our hands dirty and work to help the people. And if they became Muslim, that wasn't our business. Allah makes Muslims. We don't.

Sister Yasmine:

Okay, so the question is, where do you think the Ummah's disconnect has come from, where there are these three brothers that maybe weren't from the same family but shared the same spirit? And you were able to create Alianza. And then looking at our generation, where is the disconnect? Why haven't we necessarily been able to replicate it?

Yahya Figueroa:

Yeah, I know. Well, anyway, I would attribute that to this thing called hyper-individualism. There's a disconnect between the older generation and the younger generation. I also blame the cut and paste generation, the Google generation, for separating us even further.

Audience Member:

Teach, brother.

Yahya Figueroa:

These are some of the things that I can look at immediately, and we can agree upon them. They have not worked in our best interest. And it's sad. I think that's part of the fitna that we're living in. We're living in certain serious, critical times. We've seen strange behaviors. We see our boys becoming effeminized with their pants drawn almost beneath their ankles. There's some strange stuff going on. I remember when we became Muslims, if a sister took Shahada, she would be married within four days. And we're talking about kids, 17, 18, 19. Today it's like it's not like that. So, I don't know. It's very complicated. How can we solve that? We're going to have to put our heads together and consult one another to find the answers. I certainly don't know. I am confused. I don't understand the Millennials. And now Generation X, and Generation Z, I don't understand them. There is a disconnect. Nobody wants to read books anymore. The younger generation doesn't want to read. I have kids that are in college. They don't read. I don't understand it. We're living in some strange times.

Audience Member:

I appreciate your honesty.

Sister Yasmine:

So, the answer is with Allah, and we'll continue to ask Him to send us guidance. We're going to close this program, and I'm going to need the blessings of His bendicion, His prayer be showered on all of us and all of those who helped found and support Alianza Islamica in the beginning, the middle and then the continuation with especially our dear brother, Ibrahim Gonzalez. May the blessings be multiplied many times over and showered onto him and all of us and the children and the great grandchildren and beyond for Alianza Islamica and all the communities as well.

What Legacy Do I Leave

By Yahya Figueroa

April 8, 2017, Alianza Islamica

Recently, I pared the Islamic section of an old cemetery. My father is there. It is a beautiful, peaceful place with hundreds, maybe thousands of Muslim tombstones. Some simple, others ornate, yet each one has a quick synopsis of life. They all have a few Qur'anic verses, some have a crescent and star, and others display "Please pray Fatiha." As I made my rounds as close to death as we may get while still alive, I wondered how I could be proud of my sins and many shortcomings after being guided. I will take the advice of Islam and hide them and pray as my Lord will slightly cover them up here as he will do it again at judgment time.

How can I squeeze in what stood out in this Islamic life? Should I put the books I've read, the friendships, the marriages, some good, some failed, the heartbreaks, the failures, or accomplishments? Student of history, defender of Latino heritage, and amateur musician. What will sum up in a few lines what I want future people to pass by and say, "That's great!". Well, for right now, I am a draft open to change. I came to Islam in my youth, seeking spiritual enlightenment and fuller social justice and racial, ethnic equality. I embraced Sunnism and never swerved from it, although the times were wicked and misguided with countless cults. I never left my Sunni path, realizing that true Sunnism included mainline Sufism. I knew that the great masters of the inner path led by Abdul-Qadir Jilani and all of the other Sunni leaders were right and true.

I tried to protect and help Muslims and all decent people. I know that I was a grave sinner, but I knew even more that I have a greater Lord Almighty who overlooks and forgives again and again. I wish I had organized my time here better, and if I could do it again, I would have memorized the Quran. I would have spent more time in Mecca and Medina. I would have been more tolerant and kinder yet tougher on myself, less on others. As you see, I already need seven or eight stones, and the inscriptions are very expensive. They charge by the letter.

In a nutshell, I would say I believed in all this stuff at the end of the day. I believed in the Hereafter, The Resurrection, Heaven, and Hell. I firmly believed in the Lord of everything, in the Revealed Book, on Creation, Angels, the Devil, and that the ancient teachings of the Old and New Testaments confirmed in the Quran. They are the most profound truths of my life.

It takes a lifetime to go through all of this. Fads come and go. Ideologies and cults are a dime a dozen, but our religious foundation is the deepest part. Yes, I do believe in it all, and now I've just got to hold on and get ready to make this same cemetery my home until the end of the world.

A final thought I want to be inscribed on my stone that a former ghetto dweller dared to think he knew better than all the big-shot philosophers and silly scholars who couldn't put this story together, those who failed to recognize the Prophethood of Muhammad and truth of the Quran. That despite all their brilliance, they were trapped in word games and chasing after cheap thrills. Whatever it was that God put into our confused heads, we should treasure and gratefully hold on to every day.

A final note to the Muslims of today. Beware of the fame seekers, the glory hunters, the poster crowd. However, I may be admonishing myself. Maybe, I'm a little jealous.

Today, everyone is celebrating the work of the genius Imam Al Ghazali, and rightfully so. We had a terrible translation of the same book 40 years ago as kids. We would try to figure out what the great imam was getting at, but one of the main thrusts of his work was to avoid fame and glory, that the worst thing you can do is to profit from religion for worldly purposes. We figured that out from our beat-up cheap copies. Ironically, Imam Al Ghazali taught Sufi Islam to get away from the world. Today his teachings are being used for the opposite purpose.

Well, as I said, I m preaching to myself, and it looks like I've filled a couple of full sections of the cemetery with my tombstones. Final note, most of my family – two sisters, mother, and father – all accepted Islam from the worst example possible, me, which proves the greatness of God Almighty. Oh, don't forget the next generation is waiting for you to come and go.

A Conversation on December 13, 2020

(On Sunday, December 13th, 2020, Alianza Islamica members Peter Robasa, Mustafa Rivera, and Ramon (Rahim) Ocasio met for breakfast at George's Restaurant in The Bronx, New York.)

Peter Robasa:

The story of how I came across Alianza Islamica began when I went to the mosque to take shahadah. I had heard about Islam, the concept of monotheism, and the seerah, that is, the history of the Prophet, and I was intrigued. I said to myself, "You know what, this is the right way." So, I went to the mosque to take Shahada one day, and a Muslim brother asked me where I was from. I told him I was from Puerto Rico. He said, "Well, you might want to meet someone. In fact, he's calling the adhan right now.

That guy was Mikail, Mikhail Marrero. After he calls the adhan, which he did quite beautifully, I spoke to him afterward, and he recommended I go to Alianza Islamica. I asked him what that was, and he said it was a Latino-based organization, and they were propagating Islam in the Barrio. I remember that day I didn't leave the mosque until Mikail went through the Fatiha and a couple of surahs of the Qur'an. The first week that I went to the mosque, I met some of the brothers. I can particularly remember Yahya Figueroa telling whoever was there, "Come on, let's go. We gotta go." I thought I was going to prayer and some religious ritual. He took us all to a funeral.

I'm like, "What am I doing here, man? Is this Islam?" It turned out he had us participate in a janazah (Islamic funeral) for a brother who passed away, and I was at a loss. I didn't know what a janazah was at the time. He gave us instructions on washing the body, praying over the body, anointing the body, and wrapping the body. I was dumbfounded because I didn't know what I had gotten into. I'm looking at this and saying, "Well, maybe this is just a one-time experience, something that happens once in a while."

It turns out the next time I came, the same thing happened. As I participated in the ritual, I happened to see the deceased man's young son. He was crying. But what brought tears to him was how we were handling his father's body, how delicately we worked, and how much love and compassion we gave to him. At that point, the janazah made sense to me as a Muslim. We were preparing someone for the afterlife.

I became more engaged with Alianza and the brothers in the mosque. I was once given instructions to vacuum the mosque and to clean the toilet, and I'm looking at this and thinking, "What kind of Islam is this?".

I realized later that it was a significant part, but I didn't know it at the time. I didn't see Islam as an organization or as a process. I always saw the results: five prayers, fasting, and that's what intrigued me. But I never dove into the fact that these things are part of the process of how a community evolves. There were brothers within the organization that were so sincere, so dedicated, that they would give their arm for you, who were hungry but would share their food. They were brothers who collectively participated in drug programs, rehab programs, food programs. They serviced the community and dealt with other organizations, such as the police department and interfaith organizations. In the process of all this, you develop relationships with the brothers.

In fact, I would remember telling you, Rahim, that, at one point, I was embarrassed and ashamed of how some of the brothers were so sincere. I came from a law enforcement background with my ego, thinking I had status and a better position. But when I was around them, I noticed their piety and sincerity and how true they were to themselves. Despite their economic situation, health condition, and many other circumstances, brotherhood and unity meant more than anything. I hadn't understood that because I've never lived it. I've never really lived within an organization, within a body of people, which subscribed to the belief in One God and the Prophet Muhammad as His Messenger (peace be upon him). We evolved as a community, as a brotherhood, and there were aqiqahs and eids, all part of Islamic tradition and yet identifiable within my Latino culture.

Rahim Ocasio:

Mustafa, you could dive in anytime.

Mustafa Rivera:

Well, I remember meeting Yahya in a different environment that had nothing to do with Islam. He was a Muslim. I wasn't. We were just part of something else with him and me. And there was this brother he used to hang out with who I became very close to named Yusef.

I remember just one day being in a place where I felt spiritually bankrupt. I was doing some reflection and introspection about a bad experience that I had. I was just doing some soul searching, and I immediately came to the conclusion, a realization that something was missing in my life. And I think that what I was looking for was some spirituality, maybe a conscious contact with a God of my understanding.

Being brought up as a Catholic, a so-called Catholic, I never really identified with Catholicism. There were a lot of things I didn't understand about it. And growing up as a child, God was always a punishing God. There was constant castigation, so to speak. So, I was going through that experience when I came in contact with this brother Yusef, Yahya's friend. One night, I was home watching TV, and I saw a documentary on the history of Islamic Spain. And in that documentary, I learned what Islam is all about and how it was practiced back then.

It dealt with the Moors, the Reconquista, Queen Isabella, King Ferdinand, and Islam's fall in Andalusia. The Muslims ruled for 800 years, and I just saw a direct link between the culture that I grew up with and that history. I was strongly attracted to that.

I shared that with Yahya at some point, and we started talking about Islam, and I had a strong attraction to what he had to say. I took my shahada at his house, his mother's house, in the projects when she was still alive. Shortly after that, there was another group of us. I don't necessarily want to call it an organization, and it was just something apart from Islam. That's where Amin took his shahada, and Khalil started coming around. Khalil and Yahya knew each other from visiting the mosques in Brooklyn.

Abdul Hameed took his shahada. He was one of the bodies that we did a janazah for. And by the way, the brother that you're talking about, Peter, was Abdullahi's brother-in-law. And the young boy was his son, Huey Dunbar, the famous singer.

Rahim Ocasio:

Yes. And that was at the funeral parlor on 116th Street.

Mustafa Rivera:

Yeah. Yeah.

The funeral director was an Irish guy named Brian. Anyway, we did a few janazahs there. But getting back, Suleyman took shahada, and a few of us were very interested in Islam. We would hang out together, fast together. We were going down to Metro-North, and you'd give us classes on aqidah (Islamic creed) and fiqh (Islamic law).

We had classes on fiqh. We did classes on Tauhid Ar Rububiyya and Tauhid Al Asma wa Sifat and fasted together. Then they had the idea of reviving Alianza Islamica. Alianza Islamica was initiated many years before, as an outgrowth of the organization that you were a part of in Washington, DC.

Rahim Ocasio:

The Islamic Party in North America.

Mustafa Rivera:

Right. The Islamic Party. I don't know if it's safe to say that Alianza Islamica was an offshoot of that.

Rahim Ocasio:

If you look at the by-laws for the 501-C3, it was copied and pasted from the Islamic party's constitution. That's where you get that organizational structure and the whole idea of being an organized movement instead of just being a masjid group, where people just came in and out. It was a movement organized for a purpose, to serve the community and to make Islam a reality for people in the streets.

Mustafa Rivera:

So eventually, those by-laws were put into place. Alianza became a 501-C3 nonprofit organization. We rented this space and had meetings, classes, and jumahs there, small as it was. We were very involved with community activism and had an excellent relationship with the New York Police Department's Community Affairs Division.

I remember giving them sensitivity classes on their roll call. I would tell them what Islam was and the difference between what Sunni Muslims believe and what the Nation of Islam believes because we didn't want them to be confused about who we were. And you know we challenged the drug dealers.

We tried to do everything in as loving a manner as possible. There were times when we fed the community, had GED classes, aside from our Islamic activities. Then there was the purchase of the building and the move to the South Bronx.

But I had a wonderful experience in Islam, and we've always maintained a certain level of unity. Case in point, here we are, all these years later. Alianza Islamica, as an entity, as a physical building, hasn't existed for quite some time. But somehow, someway, we still managed to stay together.

Rahim Ocasio:

I want to make a point regarding that. I have that with the people from Alianza, and I have that with the people from the Islamic party. I could see guys from the Islamic party and feel that sense of brotherhood, just because we shared something. I'll tell you how strong it is. When I was in the Islamic party, we would line up for salah, three or four guys in the row to the right of me. I could hear a guy come in and join the line on the right and know exactly who it was. Four or five guys down, I could tell who entered the line! That's how close. When you are part of an organization and strive together, you maintain these "enlaces" of brotherhood that just doesn't fritter away.

Mustafa Rivera:

If you're spiritually in tune with your brother, you could sense when one of your brothers is going through difficulties. You could truly sense they're being challenged or struggling, wherever that brother may be.

There were a lot of other brothers. There was Ali, Mikail,

Rahim Ocasio:

Ali Cruzado

Mustafa Rivera:

Dawud Cirillo, who came around occasionally, Dawud Khalil's brother, Salif, Abu Muhammad, and the sisters as well, like Safiyya.

Rahim Ocasio:

Shair, Muhammad Omerjee.

Mustafa Rivera:

Yeah, right. Shair. And who was the brother from Spain?

Rahim Ocasio:

I think his name was Ali.

Mustafa Rivera:

No. His name was Ahmad.

Rahim Ocasio:

I remember he used to hang around after juma,

Peter Robasa:

And who was the older brother with the glasses and the beard? He was from Puerto Rico.

Rahim Ocasio:

Are you talking about the mathematician? Beautiful brother.

Mustafa Rivera:

And there was the tall African American brother who used to do security with us. And Muhammad Mendez.

And Safiyya's husband, the redhead, Idris. Yes, there were a lot of us. There were so many people that came and went.

Peter Robasa:

Special recognition and acknowledgment to all the brothers and sisters of Alianza. But I want to give a special nod to Yahya Abdul Latif Figueroa, Director of Alianza Islamica, leader, mentor, and guide. I'm pointing that out because, often, we read books about prominent people in history. And I was one of those brothers who read and thought about all I read in those books, especially when it came to the Prophet Muhammad (may peace be upon him). As my experience evolved in Alianza Islamica and all the brothers and sisters Mustafa mentioned, I started evaluating the association with leadership. I came to the conclusion that, though I've read about people in pages of history, I've never experienced a leader on a day-to-day basis. He was compassionate to all, whether consoling those grieving at janazahs or to the members.

When tensions arose when there was a drug dealer at the mosque storefront who insisted on selling drugs and was reluctant to leave, we humbly came to them, wanting them to cease that behavior at that location.

At the end of the day, it came down to us dealing with the dread Jamaican guy and trying to get him out of there. I was armed at this little standoff, but unbeknownst to me, so was Yahya, and so was he. We didn't know each of us was armed.

We kept insisting, and this guy was not getting the message. It was a standoff. Ultimately, the guy had to leave. I say that I saw Yahya Figueroa model all aspects of courtesy and trying to do it in a fashion that someone could understand.

When it came to ritual or promoting Islam, or going to other organizations as a body, Yahya Figueroa always led in a compassionate and yet assertive way. More importantly, it was dignified. He always reminded us of the importance of autonomy, the importance of keeping your head high as a people and having an identity within Islam's culture.

Rahim Ocasio:

Let me tell you something to give you a little insight into Yahya. I don't know if it was at that particular time or another, but he told me he was armed and confronted a drug dealer or dealers. He probably didn't show it, but he told me his hands were shaking. The courageous guy is not the guy who doesn't feel any fear, but the one who fears yet still manages to do what must be done.

Peter Robasa:

That's a good point.

We had our organizational goals, calling to interfaith, marching in the Muslim Day parade, we used to go to other masjids, engaged in dialogue, and did security for various places.

Mustafa Rivera:

We were part of the Muslim Security Force in New York City led by Ali Abdul Kareem from Masjid At-Taqwa in Brooklyn. We would have meetings at Taqwa discussing issues that were taking place around the city and providing various security details for multiple clients.

Peter Robasa:

Not to mention Castro when he came into town. And what was the name of that church?

Mustafa Rivera:

Riverside Church. Yahya led the security of that scene for Alianza Islamica. We all had walkie talkies, and we ensured nothing happened to Castro on his watch.

Mustafa Rivera:

We forgot to mention Ibrahim Gonzalez, who Ocasio knows better than I do. You guys had a lot of history together when you were kids.

Rahim Ocasio:

I met him when he was, like, 12. I've known Yahya since he was 13.

Mustafa Rivera:

And you guys were very much involved with other organizations, and Ibrahim, he was.

Rahim Ocasio:

Ibrahim was the guy who would make the call for us to do security at campus takeovers during the days that we were doing things like that. And he was, like, 15 years old. We would do the first watch. Every time we took over a university campus building, we would, for some reason, wind up on the first watch.

Peter Robasa:

It's funny, one thing that was very dear to me from a family point of view. When someone showed up at Alianza Islamica and had issues with drugs, Yahya would make it second nature to accept them as they are, despite their addictions and backgrounds. They were received with open arms and given food, given clothes, and provided shelter.

If a sister showed up in promiscuous attire, it was incumbent on us not to judge, condemn or criticize, but give her over to the sisters where she could start her reformation if you will. Many events took place - feeding the community, giving away clothes. Those were the little things that meant so much to me. It was like an indicator that I was in the right place with the right people at the right time because everyone who participated, all the brothers and sisters who participated, were selfless.

And in the process, Yahya didn't have to tell us much about our egos. We kind of found out in that same process, and when our egos flared up, where we would be self-righteous or self-indulgent, he would remind us that this is a collective and to get to our goal, we would have to do it as a collective moving forward.

It made me have a love for the members of Alianza Islamica. When you have a family, everybody shows up differently every time. And it develops a sense of compassion for each other. And, you know, this is not to say that emotions didn't flare up from an organic standpoint. They did. But we had each other to lean on. I've never been with a group of people that saw past each other's egos to the point where they still were always there with open arms. It is easy to judge somebody when they show up with their baggage. But it was customary to discard that and just move forward.

There were times when only a handful of people showed up. And in many cases, it was a handful of people supporting Alianza Islamica despite, on paper, having a huge membership. There were periods where you could easily complain, criticize, and play the victim. But Yahya taught us that this is a remnant of Sahabah stuff, and I could identify with it. That's why I go back to reading about Islam in terms of its historical context, understanding the Sahabah's role and what I experienced with Alianza Islamica. There were few people at times holding it down until others came, but there was no finger-pointing even though you may have had a right to do so. At the end of the day, you forgave that, too. We picked each other up, had love for each other, and were very supportive. That gave me a glimpse of what the Sahabahs may have experienced.

We held Islam's banner as the first Latino Muslim-based organization to put Islam on the map in a Latino community. I was fortunate, blessed, and honored to have done that with these pioneers, such as Yahya Figueroa, Rahim Ocasio, Ibrahim Gonzalez, and Abdulahi. You guys were the foundation. One of the reasons I say that is because you guys had degrees. No one knew. I didn't know Yahya's credentials. I didn't know your credentials.

Rahim Ocasio:

It didn't matter.

It didn't matter. But that's the point.

Rahim Ocasio:

I never told anybody.

So, your service spoke for your credentials. And then the awareness of your academic credentials came later. I told you this before. It took me a while to realize what you were offering us in terms of scholarly sources, explaining it to us even though we may not have been there yet because we were so involved in service. I know now how much of a blessing that was, Rahim, because it fortifies your Islam. And Abdullahi and Yahya provided direction.

This is my opinion. No matter what scholarly elements they quote, any organization in terms of leadership must be fortified by implementation at the end of the day. It must have a sense of experience. You all brought that to us.

Rahim Ocasio:

Do you want to know the shocker?

Up to now, there has never been an organization like Alianza Islamica.

None of the Latino Muslim organizations that have come up have even come close to Alianza Islamica. None has duplicated what we did, and, to me, that's a freaking shock.

All of us were part of something so unique. I was recently interviewed by a guy writing a paper he intends to publish on Latino-Muslim movements and organizations in America. He looked at every one of the movements and organizations and said nothing and no one has duplicated Alianza Islamica. You're part of an historic event that has yet to be duplicated.

Peter Robasa:

Let me say something about Mustafa Rivera before he leaves. He exhibited what a lot of us, perhaps, didn't say but felt. We all felt protected when Mustafa Rivera was around.

Rahim Ocasio:

He was the muscle. He was the muscle of Alianza Islamica. People felt secure around him.

Peter Robasa:

You just automatically felt secure around him. On top of that, he was direct. He was sincere, sincere with himself first before anyone else. When he did assert himself, he was firm. And when he wanted to give you clarity, you accepted it because he was hard on himself before being hard on others. And when it came time to take the initiative, he went forward. I only say that because we read about the Sahabah and Umar and only imagine what it would be like to have an Umar at Yahya's side on call.

Rahim Ocasio:

He was Yahya's go-to person.

Peter Robasa:

Correct.

I love to equate things to my experience and attribute it to what the Sahabah has done. I saw an indication of the Sahabah in Mustafa Rivera. And Yahya could depend on being fortified by him. In Yahya's absence, Mustafa Rivera was in charge because he knew that not only would the flock be protected, but that there was someone qualified to lead and sustain Alianza Islamica.

Rahim Ocasio:

You're saying that he's going to be enshrined in the historical record.

Peter Robasa:

Amin, Amin, Amin

Mustafa Rivera:

The bottom line is that the beauty of Alianza Islamica, and whatever part we played, was fundamentally spiritual. You know, as you said earlier, this was a "we" thing, and none of us are perfect. We all have defects of character. We all have shortcomings.

So aside from my relationship with Allah, I could not have done a lot of what I so-called did if it weren't for the body of Alianza Islamica, for the members of Alianza Islamica. My journey in Islam was dependent on you all and dependent on our journey together because none of us are self-reliant. We depend on a power greater than us, that being Allah. I don't think that any one of us would've endured a lot of what we endured without each other. It was through unity, the unity that came with the body of Alianza.

You talked about forgiveness and egos. The unity of Alianza kept us all in check. There was a certain level of accountability. That accountability, trust, and bond that we have with each other, not only with respect to Alianza Islamica but any organization looking to flourish, whether spiritually or whatever, if we don't have that, then we have nothing. We have nothing.

So, with regards to Yahya, Rahim, Ibrahim, Abdullahi, and myself, and you, if we didn't have each other's back, or weren't each other's eyes and ears, it would have all been for nothing. It was beautiful. It's historical. And all of us have a place in that history.

Rahim Ocasio:

And regardless of anything, we will still maintain this brotherhood.

Mustafa Rivera:

Right, exactly.

Peter Robasa:

To add to what Mustafa said on how a body moves as an organization integrating itself with other organizations. I used to see how Yahya engaged with Masjid Taqwa, in the Bronx and Brooklyn and with MIB on 113th Street and the masjid on 116th Street. They were easier to deal with as they were of African American descent. Culturally and socially, we had some of the same issues.

However, we engaged with other groups, such as the Pakistanis and other immigrant groups. And to be quite honest, we weren't widely accepted. You could see on interaction that there was a sense, a condescending sense, that they were superior to us in terms of academic credentials. Still, they were often unaware of what we were doing in the community and its impact, according to prophetic insight. Had they known, they would have treated us differently.

However, I'll give you a case in point. On 107th Street, Alianza's building was owned by a Muslim immigrant doctor who later marched in the Muslim Day Parade as the Grand Marshal. And yet, he was the one trying to evict us.

And he knew what we were doing in the community. Yet, it didn't stop him. And the only reason I'm mentioning it is to show how we dealt with those types of situations. Yahya easily could have said "Off with his head" and deal with him in a very aggressive manner. He didn't mean it literally but dealing with him in the same aggressive manner and level of malice.

The fact is, he said to deal with it with dignity, a sense of refinement, a sense of compassion, and love, and to not deviate from the direction we were heading. At our fundraisers, we were looked upon as aliens newly come into Islam, but they didn't properly assess our work until they heard some of the brothers and sisters speak and reference that body of work.

Mustafa Rivera:

Well, we've got to call it for what it is. Many Arabs did not accept us because, like my mother used to say, "Todo empieza y termina contigo", everything begins and ends with you. They didn't look at Islam as a way of life. They looked at it as a cultural custom from a nationalistic perspective. They saw us as not of their nationality and had no respect for us. I encountered very few Arab Muslims who did have some respect for us. And they admired the fact that we were involved in the things that we were involved in, but most of them had it written all over their face.

Rahim Ocasio:

And what about the issue of las mujeres, our women married to Arabs coming to Yahya because they were abusada?

Mustafa Rivera:

Yes, there was the young lady, I forgot her name from the Bronx.

And the funny thing is, we identified with it because we saw some of that in our culture growing up. Some of us saw our mothers and aunts, sisters and cousins abused, verbally, or physically. That stuff was removed, for the most part, from our way of thinking,

Rahim Ocasio:

But not removed from them, and they're supposed to be Muslim.

A lot of it had to do with the way they felt about our women.

My wife would meet Latinas married to Arabs who wouldn't teach them anything about Islam or wouldn't even let her touch the Qur'an. An Arab I know wanted to punish his wife. He told her to get on her knees. She obeyed, then she noticed him going for his belt, and she said, "You hit me with that you'll never see me again."

Peter Robasa:

So just to add to how insulting some of the immigrant Muslim community were, particularly the Arabs. They would come to Alianza Islamic specifically to ask Yahya for a wife. Never mind contributing to the Islamic effort at the center itself.

They came with an agenda in hand. And to be quite honest, now that we're old enough, we could see they were no different than any other immigrant coming here for survival but using Islam to be considered the top dog. They had no interest in serving the community or the people in need. They wanted to position themselves and their children as the top dogs. We see that coming to fruition. They are no different from other immigrants who have come here for survival, using Islam as a pretext to try to acquire things.

That's what made Alianza Islamica distinct and why I always held it dear to me.

If I had to finish on one note, it would be this. One day Al Yahya Abdul Latif Figueroa was teaching. I'm certain Mustafa was present. Salik was present. I don't remember whether it was Islamic jurisprudence or the Hadiths. And he said, "Close the books." We were taken aback by that.

He said that if all we've learned thus far is not consistent with our experience, our attainment, and the evolution of our soul, disregard it. "I don't care where it comes from, what school of Islamic thought it comes from, leave it alone. Go out there and experience, even if it's one ayat of the Quran, and live it for the rest of your life."

And he said it's about attainment, experience, and realization of the Creator. If you're going to move forward, move forward with that in mind. It'll have more of a profound effect. And so, he took all the scholarly stuff and put it on the shelf so we could have a direct experience with Allah. That would give meaning to anything Islamically that we came across. And he said the rest of it, leave it alone. And we were all taken aback by that. But he realized something. He realized that we were hiding behind Islam, we were hiding behind the literature, we were hiding behind the fiqh, we were hiding behind religion.

He took us as infants and threw us out into the world and said stop hiding. He emphasized that men make mistakes, grow, and develop. That's how we were going to evolve in Islam, by growing and not hiding behind the religion, prayers, fasting, and charity. That was common throughout the ages. Your direct experience with God is the most profound, and if you've got to make mistakes to evolve, then do so, but by no means don't you hide behind books. Or theology.

He told us to be how Allah created us with our natural fitrah and evolve and let that direct us. He cautioned us not to lose our Islamic principles but to make that the focal point of our growth and development.

Reflection on Ibrahim Gonzalez

By Rahim Ocasio

Latino Muslims are relative newcomers to the American Islamic landscape, and their history is, for the most part, unknown. But I'd like to speak of one who made a difference in how Latino Muslims are perceived, empowering them in a way that is little appreciated today: Ibrahim Gonzalez.

I met Ibrahim when he was twelve years old. He was deeply thoughtful and sensitive, and those qualities led him to a lifelong habit of looking beyond convention and a penchant for artistic expression. He developed a love for music and became a gifted guitarist, pianist, and percussionist. His sensitivity, however, also made him acutely aware of the oppressive nature of life in El Barrio. With a stubborn, unyielding sense of justice, he made it his life's mission to stand up and oppose injustice at every turn.

As a very young teenager, about 14 or 15 years old, he was organizing high schoolers as part of the Third World Students League, a Young Lords Party's mass organization. He would also manage security for campus takeovers, always willing to take the first watch and to put himself on the front line. He remained till the day he breathed his last indomitable in his commitment to the struggle for better conditions for all oppressed people.

Ibrahim became a Muslim in 1973. Like other Latino Muslims from El Barrio who came from an environment steeped in militancy and resistance, they looked to continue the struggle from an Islamic perspective. But Ibrahim was to experience frustration upon frustration. Latino Muslims were few and were dismissed by the older established Muslim groups as insignificant.

Ibrahim's sojourn highlighted this fact as an employee at ISNA headquarters in Indiana. Noticing the absence of Spanish Islamic material available, he translated a popular Islamic brochure, even preparing the printing plates. However, the ISNA brass roundly turned him down, showing absolutely no interest in proselytizing Latinos. Ibrahim was deeply hurt and troubled with the little regard his fellow Muslims held for Latinos. Before his conversion, he was a tireless worker for the rights of Latinos. Now his Muslim brothers made it abundantly clear that regarding his people, they couldn't care less. But Ibrahim was undeterred.

With the same tenacity he displayed as a teenager, he masterminded a Latino Muslim event at **El Museo del Barrio** in 1985 that made such an impact that Latino Muslims were now courted to participate in conferences and dawah programs by the same established organizations that had rebuffed and ignored them. Latinos today perhaps don't realize how significant that was. There existed a feeling in some circles that Latinos should just disappear, subsuming themselves into existing immigrant or African-American groups. But after Ibrahim's historic coup, it was clear that was never going to happen. Latino Muslims could no longer be discounted.

Ibrahim continued to be a key figure in the growth of the Latino Muslim community. He co-founded Alianza Islamica, the first Islamic organization ever to serve the needs of a Latino community. He represented Alianza Islamica at a convention sponsored by the same ISNA that had repeatedly ignored him. He became a noted radio personality, hosting two programs and was a presence on a local cable channel in the Bronx.

He never lost his love of music, going on to become a composer and producer. He loved, however, to perform onstage, often traveling the country with his quintet. Ibrahim had a profound spiritual dimension and remained to the end a faithful adherent to the Naqshabandi Sufi order.

Ibrahim Gonzalez was indeed one of the most important and influential Latino Muslims in their short history, a true pioneer. He changed the way Latino Muslims are perceived today, opening the gates toward dignity and respect, something I believe is taken for granted by the current generation. His loss was immense, but his legacy lives on. May Allah have mercy on and admit him into His Paradise. Amin.

At LALMA in Los Angeles

This is an excerpt of a speech on the history of Alianza Islamica by Rahim Ocasio presented at LALMA's Ramadan event in Los Angeles, CA on May 19, 2019.

There were problems with the Puerto Rican community because our parents associated it with the Nation of Islam. So, they felt we were leaving our culture to become African-Americans. Puerto Rican fathers would rip the khimars off their daughters' heads. It was a struggle. These were uncharted waters for us.

Over 30 years ago, Yahya and I talked about a dawah center in the heart of his El Barrio, unassuming, unpretentious, an organic part of the neighborhood, where anyone could come off the street, and hear the message of Islam. We had many starts and stops. We had trouble getting it off the ground. One day he approached me and said he wanted me to give an Aqidah class. Aqidah is Islamic creed. I had studied this recently and was able to provide this class.

At first, only two people showed up. Then four, then six, then eight.

"Wait a minute, what's going on here?" Every seat was taken, then the floor space and they just kept coming. I didn't know at the time that Yahya had been working with some Muslims that were recovering addicts. These were the people showing up. And not only did they show up and become Muslim, but they also actually wanted to make a difference. Yahya and I said (to ourselves), "Whoa. Here's an opportunity. Let's formalize this into an organization. Alianza Islamica.

Yahya went to work right away, becoming the director by consensus because he was the toughest and the sharpest of all of us. He was very aggressive and had an aggressive leadership style. He started moving things along very quickly. Anxious to implement an Islamic activist, social agenda., he secured a storefront on 107th Street, Lexington Avenue, solidly in the neighborhood where we all grew up. I want to point out here; this is the heyday of urban Islam before the great wave of Arab and South Asian immigration transformed it into a more suburban phenomenon. Completely inner-city, when masjids were storefronts and repurposed apartment buildings, not multimillion dollar complexes. That would come later.

Doctors, engineers, and PhD's were few and far between. It was more like the disadvantaged poor, former felons, and ex-drug addicts. All the early members from the Aqidah classes were Boricuas from the Barrio, so we had home-field advantage. Recovering addicts formed the bulk of the membership of Alianza Islamica and remained there at its core throughout its history. The first priority was dawah, getting the message of Islam out to the people. Alianza's style was a hands-on, face-to-face street approach. We tried different techniques and employed methods to increase exposure and interest.

Third Avenue was the main street of Spanish Harlem, so we would get all the families, women, children, and carriages, and just walk en masse. It had an effect. "Oh my God, there are Muslims everywhere." Well, we were just coming down the street and having maximum exposure. What would that do? Create interest. Conversations. People became Muslims.

The storefront was kind of low key. Sometimes a curious passerby would look in and say, "What's this?" They'd come in, and we'd get to talk to them. That way, slowly but surely, our ranks started to grow. We also, just like Marta was saying, were very concerned with religious education. So, we employed the likes of Sharif Abdul Karim, Ibrahim Abdul Aziz, and Ali Laraki. The first two were homegrown indigenous scholars. The third from Spain and were all willing to impart it to us.

Realizing that a lot of the neighborhood residents were disadvantaged, it was very important to develop programs that would give them a little head start. Some GED and ESL programs were instituted. Some of these were very successful because a good number of them went on to get their master's and doctorate degrees. Remember, these people had nothing.

We were able to take them to another level: health programs, nutritional programs, even martial arts. You need self-defense in the ghetto, and we had a martial arts program. We had a holistic approach, which included being able to beat somebody up if you had to. We also had counseling, job counseling. We created a security company to give people jobs. It's kind of tough when you have records, so those things work.

The objective was to make the Latino Muslim seem part and parcel of the community, remove the stigma of the alien, and break down barriers to the reception to Islam's message. So, a concerted effort was made to Islamize parts of our culture, like, for example, Eid celebrations. For years we were Muslims who didn't have our own events. We went to others' events, and we got tired of curry. We wanted to have something a little different.

We wanted events that featured our food. Well, as Puerto Ricans, that means we're having arroz con gandules, pasteles, and arroz con dulce. Puerto Ricans eat a lot of pernil, which is a pork roast. Puerto Ricans eat everything of the pig but the oink. We replaced it with my mother's leg of lamb innovation. She prepared it exactly the way we do with the pork dish, and it was a big hit. It's become our standard for holiday dishes.

Music is a big part of our Latino culture, especially a tropical one, so we wanted to Islamize that also. It was common in El Barrio, where I'm from, to see Puerto Ricans walking around hauling congas in a duffle bag, People would follow him knowing that he's meeting some guys for a conga jam session. Guaguanco, Bomba. We decided we could do that, too, but in an Islamic center. At our Eids, we had our congueros gather round and beat rhythms into the night. It was an open invitation to all within earshot to a new Latin expression.

The AIDS epidemic was hot in the 1990s. It grew rapidly, forcing American Muslims to deal with it. Their early reactions were positively medieval. They determined that if a Muslim died by AIDS, it was Allah's wrath, and they refused to wash the bodies. Now Yahya had attended the Second International AIDS Conference in Paris in 1986 and was very much informed and educated about AIDS and HIV. So, on his initiative, Alianza Islamica became the first Islamic organization to ritually wash bodies of Muslims who had died of AIDS. In addition, he conducted outreach programs to educate Muslims and non-Muslims alike about HIV and AIDS.

Yahya recognized that if we were going to draw Muslims from inner-city neighborhoods, many were coming broken and damaged by drugs and psychological and social ills. To address this, Alianza was instrumental in creating Brothers in Recovery, the first-ever recovery group with an Islamic bent, that's been ongoing for over 30 years. We also had to combat the problem of local drug dealers. Our neighbors were drug dealers backed by crooked cops. We weren't going to tolerate that. Alianza insisted on having good, cooperative relations with law enforcement. With a big helping hand from Captain Robert Curley and the officers of the 23rd Precinct, we cleared the drug dealers off the block.

Now some of those days were very hairy because there was a time when we were figuring we're going to get tapped. So, I remember being huddled in that storefront center waiting for something to happen. Thank God it didn't. Yahya remembers having to confront some of these drug dealers, with a gun in his hand and shaking. But he faced them and got them to back down. In the 1990s, during Rudy Giuliani's administration as mayor of New York, a slashing blood feud erupted at the Rikers Island prison between the Latin Kings, Bloods, and incarcerated Muslims. Yahya had connections with the Latin Kings and was able to broker a truce. Giuliani was so impressed with him that he offered him the chaplaincy of Rikers Island, but he refused because the job didn't have the hours he required.

Unfortunately, we were faced with problems of inordinately large cases of spousal abuse, overwhelmingly in marriages of Latinas to Arabs. There's an evident predilection for Latinas among Arabs, especially Puerto Ricans because they're American citizens. And we had a deluge of verbal and physical abuse incidents that forced Alianza to be a haven, offering assistance and badly needed counseling services. Unfortunately, in recent meetings with Latino Muslim leaders, it has become evident the problem persists unabated. It's a big problem.

In the mid-nineties, Alianza accepted an invitation by a prominent Indian Muslim to move to a building nearby.

He had a problem with drug-dealing tenants, too. They were from the Jamaican Posse, known for killing whole families. He was hoping to get our assistance to get rid of them. We took the opportunity because the space he offered was larger, and we established La Mezquita del Barrio, the first Latino community-based masjid on the East Coast, perhaps in the country, that we were aware of.

Finally, there was a place where it was possible for Latinos to come and hear khutbahs in their native tongue, ending years of feeling left out and marginalized. That's something I would like to point out. We wanted our own place, not tenants of other people's masjids, following their rules. We wanted to do what we had to do, and to initiate the programs we wanted. We had to have our own place. There was no compromise there. What I see too much these days are people feeling very comfortable as tenants in somebody else's house. I say, if you really want to do some serious work, the kind of stuff we're talking about, you've got to be on your own.

That was a milestone for us. Now we could serve Latinos in a way that the Islamic Cultural Center, which was just 10 blocks away, could never do. There, if a person came in looking like you or me and asked, "What is this place?", they'd throw you out instead of being welcoming. The Islamic Center was not the place to go. We had to have our own place because we wanted to bring people in and not have them thrown out or turned away from Islam.

Unfortunately, relations between Alianza and the building owner deteriorated.

We effectively expelled the drug dealers, and he didn't need us anymore. So, he didn't give us any services at all. We fought with him to get them done. Eventually, we were out. He was later seen marching as Grand Marshall of the Muslim Day parade down Madison Avenue. The irony.

We moved in 2000 to Alexander Avenue in the Bronx, but torn from its roots, it was never the same. Our roots were in El Barrio, and in the Bronx, we were in no man's land. It started fading, fading, fading away, and in 2005 there was a fire, which reduced to ash our final resting place.

We're now a historical footnote, kept alive by guys like Juan Galvan, who created a website called alianzaislamica.org. We threw everything we had at him, which is not much. But, Alhamdulillah, he faithfully keeps it and reproduces it. By the way, he's come out with a book called *Latino Muslims: Our Journeys to Islam*, which is groundbreaking. It's a must-read for anyone.

Okay. I see my time is going. And I hate to see a stop sign. And I don't even want to see the two-minute sign. So, I'm going to end with an excerpt from an editorial I wrote for the premier issue of the journal Alianza Islamica. And I'd like to read it for you. And that would be my conclusion.

"In this country, Latino Muslims are still few in numbers, but they're raising a considerable share of eyebrows when spotted on subways, at department stores, or while strolling through the park with their families. In some quarters, mouths still drop, and jaws become slack with amazement that a Latino could be a Muslim.

When non-Muslims, curiosity aroused, ask us about our religion, oftentimes there is a titillating streak of excitement in the air. The lure of the daring, the bold, the new is there to awaken a whole new generation to their lost heritage. We, therefore, urge our readers to plunge headlong into the real-life human drama, where the souls of men are at stake;

we urge you to spread this message by word, deed, and example. And, finally, we urge all to band together to recreate that beautiful sense of pop-eyed wonder as a people, heretofore despised and rejected, assume their rightful place in the family of man as vicegerents of the Lord and Master of all the worlds.

Alianza Islamica – Oasis in El Barrio

February 17, 2017, Alianza Islamica

By Jorge "Fabel" Pabon

As Salaamu Alaikum wa Rahmatullahi wa Barakatu,

Alianza Islamica helped form the Muslim I am today. After embracing Islam in August of 1989, I began to mosque hop (going from one mosque to another) to find my rightful place in an Islamic community. My journey began with visits to Masjid Taqwa Wa Jihad in the Bronx, Masjid Malcolm Shabazz in Harlem, the Islamic Center on 72nd, and on 96th street, and the Mosque of Islamic Brotherhood in Harlem. I also visited several mosques in Brooklyn in search of a spiritual home base and family. I was a new shahada and was soaking in tons of information regarding the deen of Islam. I read many books, viewed a fair number of videos, and spoke to many Muslims about the faith. I was gradually becoming more acquainted with my new spiritual undertaking. At this point, the majority of my influences were African-American Muslims. Transitioning from a somewhat reckless pre-Muslim aggressive lifestyle in NYC's streets, I was finally on my way towards a path of peace and purpose.

Still, in search of a spiritual home, I started to spend more time learning principles of Islam at the Mosque of Islamic Brotherhood. The Imam at M.I.B., Al-Hajj Talib Abdur-Rashid, was facilitating several Islamic courses at the masjid. These courses helped me to understand certain concepts in Islam. I would attend the classes after I got out of work in the evenings.

One day in 1992, I was done with work and decided to eat at a Dominican-owned restaurant on 105th street and

Lexington Avenue. Once I had eaten my dinner, I started walking uptown on Lexington Ave. Two blocks into my walk, between 107th & 108th street, I saw a storefront with a sign that read ALIANZA ISLAMICA INC. I was amazed that I had never seen this place. I cased it from outside, looking through the storefront window. I couldn't believe my eyes! There seemed to be Puerto Rican Muslims inside the center. At this point, I only knew Puerto Ricans who were part of the 5% Nation and members of Dr. York's Ansaaru Allah Community, both of which I studied before embracing Islam. Finally, I wanted to go inside and further investigate, so I knocked on the door wearing my Universal Zulu Nation patches/colors and a Puerto Rican flag on the front of my jacket. I was warmly greeted, and politely asked to enter. It seemed as if I walked into an oasis in the middle of El Barrio! I immediately felt a sense of commonality and belonging. I had no idea that Alianza Islamica existed and had been formulating since the 1970s. This was all new to me. After breaking bread with some of the brothers in English, Spanish & Spanglish, I felt I found my new Muslim family.

My visits to Alianza Islamica intensified as I started taking Islamic courses and getting involved with their social services and various aspects of their mission. The courses were very educational and helped me to understand my identity as a Nuyorican (New Yorker of Puerto Rican descent) Muslim. This was very important as many reverts were becoming Arabized. They felt they had to adopt Arab culture and dress – confusing one culture (of many) with the religion, hence losing their cultural identity. Alianza Islamica introduced me to the studies of the Moors in Spain (Andalusia). I immediately began to connect our cultural dots and understood our deeper Islamic inheritance while maintaining my Nuyorican identity. As a member of the Universal Zulu Nation, I was already involved in social justice and community activism. Alianza Islamica also served the community in many ways. It was a natural progression for me to help them in these efforts. I was pleased to see the multitude of services they provided for the community (for both Muslims and non-Muslims). This included Islamic studies, spiritual counseling, family counseling, GED programs, self-defense courses, sewing courses, HIV support and awareness, Puerto Rican studies, nutrition courses, survival courses, support for battered women, security services, neighborhood watch (taking a stance against the neighborhood drug dealers), Millati Islami services, administering shahadas, marriages, aqiqahs, janazahs, Eid celebrations, and community events. The list goes on & on. Though limited in space, Alianza Islamica generated an unbelievable amount of activity. Alianza Islamica was a force to be reckoned with.

I quickly started to assume responsibilities within the ranks at Alianza Islamica. As an artist, I assisted with making signs, designs, banners, etc. As a dancer and entertainer, I helped with some of the talent and specific activities at our Eid celebrations. I also began to videotape and document some of our activities. Eventually, I became a member of Alianza Islamica's planning committee and shura. We planned our weekly events, which included fundraising operations, community activities, building strategies, etc. I was honored to serve in this capacity and did all I could to support our cause.

My wife and I were married at Alianza Islamica. Several of my close friends took their shahada (embraced Islam) there. It was a haven for us. The space was always vibrant and full of activity. Babies were born, and brothers & sisters passed/transitioned. The cycles of life were in motion and revolved around our humble Islamic Center and Masjid. We were/are family in many regards. Although we no longer have a physical space, Alianza Islamica lives in each of the members who continue to hold our mission close to their hearts. We made history by becoming the first Spanish-Speaking Islamic Center and Mosque in Spanish Harlem. We continue to do so. May Allah (swt) guide and protect us throughout our journey and service to our communities.

I want to thank the leadership within Alianza Islamica for all they taught me. In particular, Hajj Yahya Figueroa Abdul-Latif, Muhammad Ibn Americo Mendez, Abdullahi Rodriguez, Rahim Ocasio, Amin Madera, Ibrahim Gonzalez, Shaykh Ali Laraki and Sister Maryam. I pray that Allah is pleased with their efforts and helps us preserve our history for generations to come.

Conclusion: Preserving A Legacy

Every moment that goes by becomes history. For the vast majority of those incessantly fleeting seconds, the human drama unfolds with no earthly record except those momentarily stored in ultimately perishable hearts and minds. In comparison, only a minuscule amount compared to the whole gets written down for posterity. These moments become frozen in time and are the repository of our past. They allow us to mine the nuggets of yesteryear, constantly re-defining who we are by re-discovering who we were. It is a primal urge.

The early Latino Muslim experience in New York City had no earthly record of its existence. It was tenuously stored in the aging hearts and minds of those in the sunset of life, always in constant danger of fading into the inexorable evanescence of time. Who then would know what happened? Who then would know why it mattered? Who then would care?

The foregoing presentation has touched on some of that history. It falls short of a definitive chronicle, for it could not possibly encompass the City's entire Latino Muslim experience. The thoughts, opinions, stories, and experiences presented here are skewed to the perspectives of pioneers and dreamers. As one of Alianza's founding members, I have found this to be exactly the perspective seekers want to hear. They want to know what life was like for a Latino Muslim 40 years ago: his trials, hurtles, and obstacles and how he overcame them. Or succumbed to them.

Time is not on our side. The shocking loss of one of the key players in this story, Ibrahim Gonzalez, really brought this home. Those who participated in this project have, in essence, become designated scribes, commissioned, as it were, by Allah's will, time, and circumstance to tell their story through the prism of personal experience. It may reek of subjectivity, but also of truth. It is what it was, and all have done their best to tell it as it was.

I dedicate this work to Almighty God Allah without whom nary a keystroke would be possible. And also, to those Muslim men and women who accompanied me on this momentous journey. And a special dedication to the fallen, my dear childhood friend and companion, Ibrahim Gonzalez, Amin Frenchie Madera, Muhammad Mendez, and all the others who have passed on. May Allah forgive them, have mercy on him, and admit them into His paradise.

Rahim Ocasio

Bonus Material:

A Historical Review of Bani Saqr

Prior to the appearance of Alianza Islamica, there was a Latino Muslim community in Newark, New Jersey. What follows is an account of their story from one of the few surviving members of that community and its first imam, Al-Hajj Yusuf Abdul Rahman Padilla-Alvarez

July 21, 2017, Alianza Islamica

Pioneers of the Latin American Muslims 'Conversion to Islam in North America

A historical examination Puerto Rican Muslim conversion in Newark, New Jersey, in the 1970s.

February 2016

By Al-Hajj Yusuf Abdul Rahman Padilla-Alvarez

My name is Al-Hajj Yusuf Abdul Rahman. I was born Jose Angel Padilla-Alvarez in El Corozo de Boqueron, Cabo Rojo, Puerto Rico, in 1954. My family migrated to New York then onto Newark, New Jersey, while I was still an infant. On the historical side, most Puerto Ricans migrated from Puerto Rico to New York, where they settled and worked. My uncles Antoline, Santos, and another person named Fundador, were the first Puerto Ricans to move from New York to Newark. My parents followed suit. My mother's two sisters remained in New York along with another brother.

The early days of Newark saw many immigrants arriving from the post-WWII generation. Later on, each group took to various parts of the city: the Italians to the north of Newark; the Portuguese and Polish to the east of Newark; the African-Americans to Central Newark; and the Puerto

Ricans to South Newark and the surrounding areas. There was a small contingent of immigrants from Turkey residing in North Newark amongst the Puerto Ricans on 7th Avenue and further out. They even set up a Masjid but only for themselves, in the middle of a Puerto Rican neighborhood in North Newark. They were of no assistance in the spread of Islam as most were very old and semi-retired. Rahim Bab was the key person from that group.

I grew up in the Dayton Street projects in South Newark, and later moved to Central Newark to So. 11th St. We did not live very far from Muhammad's Temple No. 25 on So. Orange Ave., at the time. I must have walked past this place over a thousand times. The Fruit of Islam (FOI) members standing in front as guards of the building had a notorious reputation as "crack troops" of the Nation of Islam (NOI). Newark was the first home of the NOI. The headquarters was later relocated to Chicago, IL.

Later, I got to meet one of the sons of their Minister in a private martial arts class. They lived three blocks from my home just off 13th Avenue. He was the head instructor who had spent eight years in Japan training in martial arts and attending school. He was very pleasant and friendly with me and took to me as one of their own. The group experienced a split, and his father was killed in front of his home. His oldest brother took over the Ministry. The three defector murderers were captured by FOI members and were beheaded by someone in the group. Their bodies were found (but not their heads) just two blocks from my home (which later became the HQ for Bani Sakr and the Jaami) in an empty lot, which became the home of the state medical university. He preached to me some version of Islam but very fundamental and slanted.

Later on, I met some local Puerto Rican friends, blood brothers, not too far from my home by the names of Ruben and Tato Agosto. There was also a younger brother by the name of David and another older brother, whose name I don't recall. David had moved to New York City, to the South Broadway area just adjacent to Chinatown, off of Canal Street with his sister. That area was known as Little Italy. It was where "The Godfather Part I" was filmed, and the New York mafia was headquartered. David died at a young age. Prone to gang warfare, he was killed by Tongs from Chinatown. The "Agosto Brothers" never converted to Islam. Ruben was the only supporter amongst the brothers, and we were as one family with them. Ruben later in life suffered losing both of his legs from an auto accident. However, he introduced me to the "Rios Brothers" in North Newark, who turned out to be my distant cousins through their mother, who was also a Padilla. I never met her husband, but his last name was "Room," just as the name of the Surah of the Quran referring to the Romans. This was an untypical Spanish name. Hispano-Roman for sure.

I recall meeting an African American brother by the name of Jaafar Abdel Mu'min (Lonnie Smith) (May Allah have mercy on him), and I forgot how we met. Still, he, in turn, introduced me to another African American brother by the name of Faqir Lillah Abdul Rahim (Daniel Hicks), who still lives. Both preached to me about Islam. It was sometime after my mother's death, around 1972, that Faqir took me to the State Street Masjid in Brooklyn, NY, for shahadah with the elderly Imam Hafiz Mahmud Maqbul (May Allah have mercy on him). I believe he was Indian. Shaykh Dawud, who was of Haitian descent, established the masjid in 1933, and called it "The Muslim Mission of America." He was elderly and still there at the time. He was famous for yelling out to the brothers before the Salatul Jumat, "I smell feet!!". State Street was replete with many immigrant Yemenis and other Arabs at the time.

Back in Newark, while living with my parents, brothers, and sister, I welcomed Jaafar to stay with me. Not long after my conversion, another Puerto Rican brother, by the name of Faruq Abdul Alim RA (Jose Hernandez), accepted Islam. I came to know him through Jaafar (May Allah have mercy on him). Soon after another by the name of (Yahya Abdul Khayyam (Juan Garcia) (may Allah have mercy on him) accepted Islam. He came through Yahya. Both accepted Islam within a year of each other. Yahya and I go back to the Young Lords Party of Newark, headed by Ramon Rivera before we, Yahya and I, were Muslim. Some time afterward, I was informed by Faqir Lillah, because he spent lots of time in New York City, that he met another Puerto Rican Muslim by the name of Ibraheem Gonzalez (may Allah have mercy on him). I did not meet Ibraheem until much later on, maybe several years at a function we were sponsoring in Newark. He later went to Egypt and spent more than ten years there then returned to the states.

Now, this is where it starts getting interesting. Both of my brothers left home, one got married, and the other set out for Vietnam. I had the place to myself along with my sister. There was lots of intrigue going about the Muslim communities in New Jersey and New York. I decided to join up with Kamil Wadud's community. Then one day, we had the Saudi Council General pass through; he gave me a look as if to say, I was in the wrong place. I had no idea that he was associated and good friends with Al-Hajj Heshaam Jaaber (may Allah have mercy on him). It truly became a world of spies. Kamil was accused of working with the CIA(?) I thought those guys operated overseas, not domestically. There were all sorts of suspicious plots and underground stuff going around.

Sometime later, Faqir Lillah came to us and told us that he met a Shaykh from Elizabeth (another town just next to Newark) who had been there for quite some time. He was Al-Hajj Heshaam Jaaber. We met him and found him to be a very eloquent speaker and "believer" who had been exposed to the Muslim's atrocities under Algeria's French occupation and had fought in that struggle against the French. Al-Hajj Heshaam had an affinity for the Saudis at the time and was instrumental at organizing the various groups in the Newark area: Baitul Khaliq headed up by Abdellah Yasin and Deenullah Masjid, headed by Al-Hajj Akal Karam. Al-Hajj Heshaam RA had spent an additional 11 years in the Muslim world before returning to the states.

Nonetheless, he had a small house close to Port Elizabeth, on Magnolia Street that we called "the Jaami," as a functional place of prayer and gathering. We frequented "the Jaami" many times, even in the worst of the bitter winters. There were many occasions that the house did not have any heating oil during the freezing winters, only an electrical floor heater, and the water was ice-cold for wudhu. Al-Hajj Jameel was the keeper and maintainer of "the Jaami," living there with his young family. We met many African American brothers who had spent 4-5 years in Mecca and returned for a brief moment before heading back; many stayed temporarily at "the Jami." Many others traveled to Saudi and Egypt and remained there never to return. Brothers such as Al-Hajj Hasan returned to Mecca and Abu Bakr Siddiq, who took his very young daughter to conclude his life in Egypt. Shuaib Muhaiman stayed in Mecca for seven years with his family but also returned.

Al-Hajj Heshaam was part of an older African American group with its roots in the founding fathers of modern African-American Islam. These were the proto-Islamic movements such as the Nation of Islam headed by Elijah Muhammad, the Moorish Science Temple, and noted personalities Marcus Garvey, Daddy Grace, and Father Divine. There was a photo on a wall of one of the survivors at the time that showed quite a few African-Americans along with Ustaz Muhamed Ezaldeen (may Allah have mercy on him) dating back to the early or mid-1930s).

Shaykh Al-Hajj Heshaam was the National Imam for the AAUAA – Adeenulllah Al-Jamia Ummiya Al-Arabiya Al-Islamia. I am not sure about the incorporation date, but it goes as far back as the early 1930s (or maybe earlier) under the leadership of Ustaz Muhamed Ezaldeen. He spent ten or more years at Al-Azhar University, Egypt. It was during the time of Kamil Ataturk and the pre-fall of the Khilafat. He, Ustaz Muhamed Ezaldeen (as the story goes), had traveled to Turkey to organize along with other Muslims an insurgent group to undermine Kamil Ataturk's attempts to eradicate the Khilafat. This would put an end to the 683-year Ottoman Empire, the longest any Muslim nation has held the Khilafat of Islam, the center of its religious and political power. Their efforts were not successful, and they fled Turkey "on foot" back to Egypt. Henry Ford had yet to invent the Model-T Ford. He eventually returned to Newark, and while preparing a place for prayer, he stepped on a nail, caught gangrene, and passed away. Daddy Grace also returned to Newark as well as Elijah Muhammad, and each went their ways.

I had the opportunity to meet some of the original remaining brothers that were still alive while in their senior years. Al-Hajj Hadi Bey (may Allah have mercy on him),

Al-Hajj Sayyid Ahmad (may Allah have mercy on him), and others lived in a small farming town in southern New Jersey called Elm, in Hammonton County. There they set up the AAUAA headquarters. The AAUAA platform was Islamic, and Ustaz Muhamed Ezaldeen taught that African-Americans were of the Arab race (which takes some explaining). Up to three generations classify themselves as such to this very day.

I preached to my cousins, the Rios Brothers, and they were my first converts. First Luqman, then Isam, Jamal then Muhammad, and later a family friend or relative named Huma (may Allah have mercy on her). Many others followed through this chain of relationships. We made no open public dawah efforts and grew organically from within; our ranks were continuously swelling. We were young, but we "believed." Unlike metropolitan and cosmopolitan New York City and Brooklyn with millions of diverse people and cultures, Newark, on the other hand, was a small city. It had no more than 350,000 people, was very porous, and it seemed as if everyone was related or connected to others in some way or another. There was no alley, street, or corner that I did not know or had not walked down.

As we grew and expanded into the predominant Catholic/Pentecostal tightly knit Puerto Rican community, other non-Muslim Puerto Ricans began to take notice. They did not like nor respect us. There were too many ties of relationships via blood and friendships that were binding everyone together (Muslim and non-Muslim). It was a powder keg. Some traditional families had become divided through religious lines.

We had non-Muslim community pillars, both political and business, through our previous relationships that kept everyone at bay. Except for a few distant areas of the city, Newark was predominantly a massive ghetto. Due to the legacy of the former Mayor Adonizio's corrupt government and the post-1960's riots, everything criminal that you could imagine was flowing throughout the Newark ghetto. The city ranked as the nation's number 1 murder capital. It was the law of the jungle for survival.

So, it was impossible to bar admission to ex-convicts and former criminals into our tight Puerto Rican Muslim community. "Conversion was a matter of Shahadah, but the transformation is a matter of time." So, there it was, weapons of all sorts flowed back and forth; buying, selling, and brokering and the non-Muslim Puerto Ricans were well aware of it. It was the equalizer. Early on, when it was just a few of us, my relatives, myself and a few friends, someone broached the subject of having an imam, and since I was the one who made the call to Islam, I was appointed imam. I had no idea what it was all about and into what I had gotten. Years later, after relocating to Texas, I found out how much I lacked by way of everything. I spent the following 18 years in Dallas at the IANT, under the Hanafi Turkish scholar and Imam, Dr. Yusuf Kazaki.

Al-Hajj Heshaam RA was inspirational, eloquent, and convincing. If you don't know the name, he presided over Al-Hajj Malik Al-Shabazz's (Malcolm X) eulogy and burial, draped in classic desert Arab abaya and ghutra when it was not fashionable to do so.

There was too much going on to recollect all the events and details. Al-Hajj Heshaam was a very clever man. He suggested to us that we call our community Bani Sakr. Although the name was Arabic and uncommon, we collectively decided to go along with it. I can't recall if Bani

Sakr was ever incorporated. Not long afterward, we got the word that the Rabitat Al-Alim Al-Islami (World Muslim League based in Mecca) was about to set up an office in New York City, and the first Secretary-General and UN representative was Dr. Ahmad Hussien "Sakr." What a coincidence! He was clean-cut and very sharp, but he didn't have a plan according to sources. So, we prepared a well thought out plan for a national Islamic organization based on the Majlis Ash-Shurah principles. Eight years later, the Muslim World League held the 1st General Assembly meeting of the Shurah Council. However, we were not invited. I went to see who of the 300-400 delegates at the hotel were and what I saw appeared to be not very religious businesspeople in expensive suits. That event was held in Elizabeth, New Jersey. Appreciation and thanks were finally rendered 16 years later by Dr. Ahmad Hussein Sakr himself at a conference in Chicago, IL. He addressed a group of 1200+ Muslim leaders from around the world on the Saudi government-sponsored post-Mecca massacre, which led to the death of 400+ pilgrims by Saudi security forces only a couple of days before the Hajj season. Supposedly most of them were Shias, but many too were Sunnis as they marched together in a procession denouncing the Kufar. He was known to the brothers and certain circles as "Big Head," solely because of the size of his head. Other than that, he was a very nice and humble brother. I was residing in Texas at the time of the Chicago occasion.

Such is the origin of our name, Bani "Sakr." It was not the result of someone's creative moment, but a play on the new MWL Secretary-General and UN representative's name. My best guess was that we were supposed to get warm and fuzzy "Rico Suave" style with the new brother in town, the man with the money. I have seen him years later at his

Islamic Center in California with Mustafa Calendario Cervantes, a Mexican brother whose grandfather was Coronal Calendario Cervantes, who was an officer in Pancho Villas liberation army. IFSO (International Federation of Students Organization), a branch of Rabitat (MWL) through their Ugandan representative Dr. Omar Kasuli, sponsored us to give dawah in Los Mochis, Sinaloa, Mexico. Mustafa's hometown was in Angostura, further down the coast. A hand full of friends of his became Muslim.

As we were making almost daily rounds to "the Jami," Al-Hajj Heshaam had also impressed us with his use of the word "Lord," referring to Allah with the words "Young Lords." We knew there was no religious relation to the two.

The Young Lords Party was socialist-based, and the top tier promulgated free-sex amongst their followers and even sharing of each other's wives. I also heard through the grapevine from a very reliable source that this went well with the rank and file, but when it occurred with the ladies and wives of the Ministers, it didn't go so well. Some say this was the cause of the breakup of the Young Lords.

Nevertheless, I don't know what I was thinking, or, for that matter, what we were thinking. But this too had something to do with the decision to go on with the name Bani Sakr.

Later or before, Al-Hajj Heshaam RA decided to have what I called an "Imam Crash Course." I don't think it was more than a dozen classes. After that crash course, I gave my first khutbah at "the Jaami."

There was a rift between us and Brother Jaafar. We parted ways, and four years later, he was found murdered with multiple stab wounds. We were very sure who did it, but the murderer fled the state never to be seen again. Time passed by, and Brother Faqir drifted into the shadows as events unfolded and played out. Al-Hajj Heshaam was inducted into the ranks of the Muslim World League as a speaker. The Iraq-Iran war kept him busy as a journalist for Islamic Press International, interviewing the Arab and Muslim Ambassadors.

While we were struggling to stay together, some of the undesirables that came into the community earlier began to create mischief in the Newark community and drew condemnation from the non-Muslim Puerto Ricans, demanding who was responsible for this group. There seemed to have been unnecessary deaths over bad business deals among specific individuals, not close to Bani Sakr's core membership. But our name was implicated. All fingers pointed at me. I had to clean up a lot of mess I didn't create nor wanted to get involved with. It was not my responsibility, but I managed.

I can't remember the number of years we lingered loosely together. Still, precious time and the informative years were passing quickly, and frustrations mounted and began to emerge amongst certain individuals within the Bani Sakr core. There were many broken promises from so-called Muslim and Arab funding sources, outside support groups, and internal disputes about the actual goals and direction of Bani Sakr began to surface.

At the time, it was a free-for-all in the greater U.S. Islamic community ripping off other Islamic communities' funding proposals. Even funding earmarked for the publishing of Qur'ans disappeared. The Arabic-speaking brokers obtained funds from Saudi and other international Islamic organizations and absconded with the badly needed monies meant for struggling communities. Indigenous

American Muslims were always looked upon as second-class Muslims. Latin American Muslims in North America were nothing to be regarded. We just didn't count or seem to exist. This attitude is still prevalent even unto today to some extent, simply because the Latin American Muslims are not properly represented in a unified way. As the fastest growing population conversion-wise, with as many as 2 million Latin American Muslims and the majority women, there is much room for abuse by the other Muslim communities, especially to the unknowing new converts. You can expect back-room marriages with no license nor blood tests, and bogus marriage certificates with close friends of the groom as representative witnesses. It's widespread in the states. Solutions and an information dissemination system should be investigated to address these abuses.

Bani Sakr was misdirected into a form of a "movement" as opposed to a "knowledge-focused" and learning community. Our religion is focused on seeking knowledge, the kind of knowledge that gets us closer to Allah.

I surmised that after the demise of Bani Sakr as an active community, what was needed was a transformational and educational effort of Islamic Ta'leem and Tartib of 10 years at the minimum of intensive teaching-learning to fully develop the minds, psychology, and souls of the North American Latino Muslims. Much was missing. Nationwide there was no framework nor infrastructure for Islamic institutional learning. It finally came but came too late for many.

Dissolution began to take root. Excessive problems mounted. There was uncalled for loss of life due to careless and irresponsible individuals, which tarnished the group's image as a whole.

In time, Bani Sakr slid into disarray, and many began to disperse. Everyone went their way, away from the community altogether. Many strayed back to pre-Islamic lifestyles and out of Islam entirely. Some died honorable deaths, and, like my cousin, Isam would put it, those who strayed died non-honorable deaths.

A few individual brothers were prospering while the more significant portion of the community was suffering financially both individually and as a group. Newark did not offer economic growth opportunities for its population. It had a stagnant economy. Without a strong family support structure, the door for hijrah had opened. That was the road I took. I eventually left Newark and headed south to Texas, where I started over. I had made the Hajj while I lived in Texas but with the brothers from Elizabeth, New Jersey. I went to Mecca again the following year for Umrah by myself.

There were other Muslim characters in our midst that were not Puerto Rican. Abdel Malik was an Italian who eventually moved to New York for greater exposure. Omar, the only African-American member, was with us almost daily until the end. I can't think of anyone else who was not Puerto Rican who was part of the original group outside of Jaafar and Faqir. Hussein, my ex-brother-in-law, was half Italian and Puerto Rican. His dad was Thomas "Tommy Gun" De la Monica, but I've never seen him with a gun.

My personal view is that we need to stop looking outside of our Latin American group for guidance and leadership. Every community in America had sought leaders from among themselves. There are surely notable scholars in the states, but we have them too and can cultivate our own. We have been around long enough and seen enough to know the correct way to teach and to move forward as Latin American nations. Most of us who have survived the early pioneering years and have lived fulfilling lives must ponder that there is a Divine reason we are still around. We need to lay down a better foundation and road map for our unique situation(s). We are not just Muslims, as in Anglo or African-American Muslims. We represent "countries."

We have our roots in distant lands, and our histories are tied to Islamic Spain, and beyond. It is not complete without it. We need to encourage our youth to make hijrah to the Islamic universities of Al-Azhar and others in the Maghrib. I do not subscribe to the Saudi firebrand of extreme, rigid, and hardline Wahhabism.

The jurisdictional (madhhab) tradition of Islamic Spain was that of the Maliki madhhab, but any of the traditional madhhabs are good enough, as they were the closest to the first generations, and thus closer and purer to the source of knowledge and faith.

In the Muslim minds of West and North Africa, Spain is considered the Maghrib, and is still considered part of the Maghrib to this day.

Of course, there is much to the story of Bani Sakr. There were many good times and experiences. There is no doubt, too many to recall. If this document were to circulate among the surviving founders, they could contribute their versions and experiences. The proof of Islam is reflected in our continued devotion to Allah, and in our love of the Prophet (peace be upon him) for showing us the way. We uphold his Sunnah as part of who we are and will always be until we meet Allah again, as Muslims.

I believe with certitude that we can outshine collectively many of the other national communities in the states and other parts of the Americas through the example of a strong brotherhood and sisterhood unified by cultural similarities and language, with purpose and as "one people" in Islam.

Allahu Waliyul Taufiq

Al-Hajj Yusuf Abdul Rahman Padilla Al-Maliki Al-Arabi Al-Andalusi At-Tijani

About Rahim Ocasio

Ramon "Rahim" Ocasio is a speaker, writer, prolific lecturer, and co-founder of *Alianza Islamica.* As a devout follower of Islam and a tireless advocate for Latino Muslims across America, Rahim is passionate about bringing the teachings of Islam to his community and amplifying their voices through his activism and speeches.

Rahim has given dozens of lectures on Islam and the legacy of Islamic Spain for institutions including New York University, Howard University, Baruch College, Boricua College, Rutgers University, Cooper Union, Northeastern University and America's Islamic Heritage Museum. He's dedicated to sharing the rich history of Islam in the Latino world, and his tireless work has led him to become a prominent and celebrated member of the Latino Muslim community.

Rahim is also the co-author and editor of the book *Alianza Islamica: Spanish Harlem s Islamic Journey,* which aims to reveal the untold story of the birth of America's best known Latino Muslim organization, along with the challenges they faced along the way. He was also a former copy editor/contributing editor for The Message magazine, in addition to a former Guidance Council member of the Washington branch of the Islamic Party of North America.

Inspired by the tumultuous civil rights activism of the 60s and 70s, Rahim Ocasio has devoted his life to tackling social issues within the Latino community, addressing poverty, and inspiring the disadvantaged with a powerful source of faith and hope through Islam. Rahim now spends his days lecturing, writing, and spending time on his family farm.

About Juan Galvan

Juan Jose Galvan advocates for the inclusion of the Latino Muslim voice in the mainstream Muslim narrative. He pushes for increased visibility of America's Latino Muslims in secular and non-secular publications. Juan has assisted dozens of students, professors, and reporters with research and has provided access to the Latino Muslim community through interviews and his writings. In 2017, he coauthored a report called *Latino Muslims in the United States: Reversion, Politics, and Islamidad.*

He has developed a growing national reputation as a content expert on the Latino Muslim community through newspaper interviews and publications. Juan has been quoted in many publications including the New York Times, the Houston Chronicle, and the Los Angeles Times. Hernán Rozemberg of the San Antonio Express-News wrote in 2005, "After becoming a Muslim, (Juan) Galvan made it his personal mission to inform the country about Latino Muslims." His first book was *Latino Muslims: Our Journeys to Islam.*

Juan is honored to work with Latino Muslim pioneer, Rahim Ocasio, to educate Muslims from all walks of life about an overlooked part of Latino Muslim history with the book, *Alianza Islamica: Spanish Harlem s Islamic Journey.* The history of Latino Muslims in the United States did not begin post 9/11 – and this book also will introduce Muslims to the beautiful story of the Bani Saqr from Newark, New Jersey in the 1970s.

Juan is a third-generation Mexican-American and graduated with recognition as a College Scholar from the University of Texas at Austin School of Business. He spent his early years hoeing cotton in the rural Texas Panhandle. You can learn more about his efforts at latinomuslim.com.